AROUND
SAVANNAH

WHERE TO GO
AND
WHAT TO DO
WITH CHILDREN

BY
GWEN MCKEE & KACEY RATTERREE

ILLUSTRATED BY
KACEY RATTERREE

First Printing, 2007

Library of Congress Catalog Card No.
2007-902561

For Additional Copies, Please Contact the Publisher:
Me and My Friend Publishers
P. O. Box 16208
Savannah, GA 31416
912-352-7086
www.savannahwithchildren.com

Printed in the United States of America by
PressWorks Printing

Maps by
Drew Martin

Typesetting and Layout by
Sylvia Lewis

ISBN No. 978-0-9642753-2-4

To our children

who inspired this book

Joe and Katie and Mary Ellen, Tom and Billy.

TABLE OF CONTENTS

Readers are advised to call sites before visiting to confirm hours, days open and admission fees.

ACKNOWLEDGEMENTS

SAVANNAH IS SPECIAL

DOWNTOWN/HISTORIC DISTRICT

EAST SAVANNAH, ISLANDS AND TYBEE

ACKNOWLEDGEMENTS

We appreciate the many people who have provided updated information and suggestions for our newly revised book. We also thank our friends and family who have helped us review the new sites added to this book.

SAVANNAH IS SPECIAL

Whether you are a native of Savannah, a newcomer, or a visitor, we think you will agree that Savannah is a special place. Graceful and magnificent live oaks shade the squares and streets of a city founded in 1733. Historic, geographic, and archaeological surprises are intertwined at many of the sites included in this book. Young visitors will delight to hear tales of pirates and shanghaied sailors, to explore forts built like castles, and to wander along nature trails. Girl Scouts making their pilgrimage to Savannah to see the birthplace of Juliette Gordon Low will discover that Savannah was also home to writer Flannery O'Connor and sculptor Ulysses Davis. Wildlife, sea life, Revolutionary and Civil War history are juxtaposed in entertaining ways.

Fortunately, there are many sites to visit in and near Savannah. Opportunities for children are plentiful, providing glimpses of life in a port city which has been a bustling hub for three centuries. We felt it was appropriate to have a book that introduces children to that which is unique to Savannah, Chatham County and surrounding counties. The book is designed to be used in many ways: to help teachers plan field trips, to introduce new families to what our community offers, to assist visitors in making the most of their stay here, and to inspire adventures for any group or occasion.

Having five children between us, we continually sought ideas for weekend and summer outings. This book represents our findings. We have had a wonderful excuse to revisit our favorite places in Savannah as well as to discover new ones. Our children enjoyed our project as they and their friends "reviewed" the sites with us. Your children and grandchildren will enjoy these youthful comments about our adventures.

We hope you will find this book "user-friendly" and that it will encourage you and your children to discover and treasure what makes Savannah special. Please visit our website, www.savannahwithchildren.com.

DOWNTOWN/HISTORIC DISTRICT

1. Battlefield Park
2. Beach Institute African-American Cultural Arts Center
3. City Market and Art Center at City Market
4. Juliette Gordon Low Birthplace
5. King-Tisdell Cottage
6. Live Oak Public Libraries
7. Massie Heritage Center: Savannah's Teaching Museum for History and Architecture
8. Negro Heritage Trail Tour
9. The Pirates' House
10. Ralph Mark Gilbert Civil Rights Museum
11. River Street and Bay Street
12. Roundhouse Railroad Museum
13. Savannah History Museum
14. Savannah National Wildlife Refuge
15. Savannah's Squares and Forsyth Park (entire map on page 5)
16. Savannah Visitor Information Center
17. Ships of the Sea Museum
18. Telfair Museum of Art
    Telfair Academy of Arts and Sciences
    and Jepson Center for the Arts
19. Mrs. Wilkes Boarding House

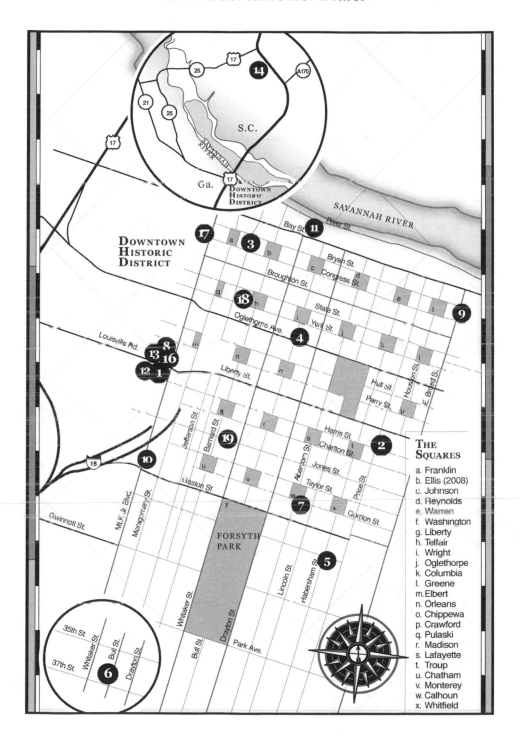

DOWNTOWN HISTORIC DISTRICT

THE SQUARES

a. Franklin
b. Ellis (2008)
c. Johnson
d. Reynolds
e. Warren
f. Washington
g. Liberty
h. Telfair
i. Wright
j. Oglethorpe
k. Columbia
l. Greene
m. Elbert
n. Orleans
o. Chippewa
p. Crawford
q. Pulaski
r. Madison
s. Lafayette
t. Troup
u. Chatham
v. Monterey
w. Calhoun
x. Whitfield

BATTLEFIELD PARK

Managed by the Coastal Heritage Society
303 Martin Luther King, Jr. Blvd.
Savannah, GA 31401
Location: SW corner of Harris Street and Martin Luther King, Jr. Blvd.
(912) 651-6825
www.chsgeorgia.org

■ ■

DAYS/HOURS OF OPERATION
Sunup to sundown

FACILITIES
Nearby at Roundhouse Railroad Museum

HINTS
* Combine with visit to Roundhouse Railroad Museum

"I like the grassy green hill."
Annie Lillian Bordeaux, age 6

"My favorite part is the gift store for children."
Thomas Bordeaux, age 5

Adjacent to the Railroad Roundhouse Museum on Harris Street is the newly excavated Spring Hill Redoubt. This Redoubt was a key battlefield position in the Siege of Savannah, 1779, where Allied American, French, and Haitian soldiers fought against British troops during the Revolutionary War. Soldiers from many nations were engaged. Polish hero General Casimir Pulaski, father of the American Cavalry, was mortally wounded in the battle.

An American flag flies above 800 markers laid in parallel rows which represent the Allied casualties from the October 9, 1779, charge against the fortified Redoubt. More detailed information on the Siege of Savannah can be found in the Savannah History Museum across the street.

Although the Redoubt offers just a brief glimpse into the Revolutionary past in Savannah, it is also a rare opportunity to envision this historic battle. So much of American history has been paved over or built upon. In this moment in time the British ruled the colonial city of Savannah.

The British evacuated Savannah on July 11, 1782, after Lord Cornwallis surrendered to George Washington at Yorktown.

Refer to pages 33 and 31 for descriptions of the nearby Savannah History Museum and Roundhouse Railroad Museum.

ACROSS

1. **In which war was this battle?**
3. **Key battlefield position**
5. **Soldiers from Britain**
7. **Where did surrender happen?**

DOWN

2. **What was the name of this battle?**
4. **Soldiers from Ireland**
6. **Who surrendered in 1782?**
8. **Who received surrender?**

BEACH INSTITUTE AFRICAN-AMERICAN CULTURAL ARTS CENTER

502 East Harris Street (entrance is on Price Street)
Savannah, GA 31401
(912) 234-8000
www.kingtisdell.org

- -

DAYS/HOURS OF OPERATION
Tuesday-Saturday: 12 noon - 5 p.m.
Closed Sunday and Monday

ADMISSION
$4 per adult
$2 per student
$2 senior citizens
There is no admission charged when
city-sponsored exhibits
are on display.

FACILITIES
Handicapped access
Parking
Restrooms
Video presentation about Ulysses Davis

HINTS
* Allow 40 minutes
* Combine with visit to King-Tisdell Cottage nearby

> "There are some amazing wood-carved statues here.
> I can't believe somebody carved these with a knife."
>
> *Joe Ratterree, age 9*

The Beach Institute was built in 1867 to house a school for newly freed
African-American children, the first such school after Reconstruction. The

school was run by the American Missionary Society and named for Alfred E. Beach, the editor of *Scientific American* and an inventor whose generosity allowed the purchase of land on which the school was built. Several years ago the Savannah College of Art and Design bought the building and donated it to the King-Tisdell Cottage Foundation. Today, the building features a permanent collection of African-American art and changing exhibits in addition to the Ulysses Davis Folk Art Collection.

Children will especially enjoy the period classroom of the 19th century A garden adjacent to the building features a fountain designed by former Savannah blacksmith Ivan Bailey. The fountain is a series of symbols in the evolution of the freedom of African-Americans. Children will enjoy looking for the symbols.

The Ulysses Davis Collection is a significant collection of over 230 wood carvings. Ulysses Davis (1913-1990) was a barber who whittled between patrons and in his spare time. His work is recognized nationally for its contribution to American folk art. Using crude tools, Davis carved intricacies that seem to defy the scope of the tools. To many of his pieces he applied tiny ornaments for texture and dimension. A few of his works are painted. Some of his carvings are decidedly religious, others political. The series of American Presidents is particularly impressive. The collection has been exhibited in the galleries and museums of major American cities. It is Savannah's good fortune that the King-Tisdell Cottage Foundation was able to purchase this collection and make the Beach Institute its permanent home.

CITY MARKET AND
ART CENTER AT CITY MARKET

Jefferson Street at West St. Julian Street
219 West Bryan Street, Suite 207
Savannah, GA 31401
(912) 232-4903
(912) 234-2327 (Art Center)
www.savannahcitymarket.com

DAYS/HOURS OF OPERATION
Monday-Saturday: 10 a.m. - 6 p.m.
Sunday: 1 p.m. - 5 p.m.
Shops, galleries and restaurants may have different hours

ADMISSION
Free

FACILITIES
Handicapped access
Pay phone
Restrooms

HINTS
* Plan a visit around mealtime
* Carriage tours begin here
* Allow 30 to 45 minutes for
  browsing; more time for eating or a carriage tour
* Call ahead about special events
* Go upstairs to visit working artists in the
  City Market Art Center

"I like to pat the horses."
Katie Ratterree, age 5

"There are some neat stores here where I like to buy things."
Joe Ratterree, age 9

The City Market is a two block area of shops, restaurants, cafés, studios, and galleries located in restored 19th century buildings surrounding a pedestrian-only section of St. Julian Street. It is nestled between Ellis Square, which was the original city market where vendors and farmers sold their wares, and Franklin Square, which was once the site of the city water tank. During the 1980s, this two block, four building area was renovated for specialty retail shops and restaurants. More recently, an art center, galleries, and artists' working studios have also located here. Brightly-striped awnings and unique signs identify the various shops and restaurants, and outdoor seating and a covered gazebo in St. Julian Street are inviting places to take a break. City Market is the origination point for the carriage tours, and the horses and buggies are always intriguing for younger children.

Inside the buildings, care was taken during renovation to leave intact much of the original structures and materials. Wide-plank wooden floors and exposed brick walls are two features that recall earlier times. The upper stories of two of the buildings are filled with artists' studios. Sculpture, printmaking, textile design, and painting are examples of the work in progress that might be glimpsed here.

A visit to City Market feels complete when centered around a meal. Dining experiences vary from a lively pizza parlor to a casual café atmosphere to more formal dining. Outdoor seating is pleasant year-round.

City Market is the site of several community cultural events. These include the Savannah Folk Music Society concert (October), Savannah Music Festival concerts (March-April), Christmas Open House with a special Saturday afternoon Christmas for Kids, and more.

The restoration of Ellis Square, one of the original four squares, marks its renewed status as a greenspace. It was once the site of the Old City Market. The Market's demolition in 1954 made way for a modern parking garage and gave rise to Historic Savannah Foundation. Recently, the garage was demolished and underground parking will be provided beneath Ellis Square.

JULIETTE GORDON LOW BIRTHPLACE NATIONAL HISTORIC LANDMARK

Owned and operated by the Girl Scouts of the USA
10 East Oglethorpe Avenue
Savannah, GA 31401
(912) 233-4501
www.girlscouts.org

■■■

DAYS/HOURS OF OPERATION
Monday, Tuesday, Thursday, Friday, Saturday: 10 a.m. - 4 p.m.
Sunday: 11 a.m. - 4 p.m.
Closed Wednesdays, November - February
Open Wednesdays, March - October: 10 a.m. - 4 p.m.
Closed some Major Holidays, including St. Patrick's Day

ADMISSION
$8 per adult, $7 registered Girl Scouts, students & children (5-20)
$25 per family (up to 2 adults, 4 children), children under 5 free
Special group programs; inquire for group reservations, rates
Prices subject to change

FACILITIES
Drink Machine
Guidebooks for sight- and hearing-impaired
Handicapped access (Elevator in main house)
Museum Store
Restrooms

HINTS
* Save time for a visit to the museum store
* Special programs are available for some groups
* Groups of 10 or more are encouraged to make advance reservations.

"You could tell our guide liked to show children
through this house. He was so funny."

Joe Ratterree, age 8

Juliette Gordon Low may be known best as the founder of the Girl Scouts, but a tour of her birthplace will surprise visitors with many of her other talents as well. Juliette, known as Daisy, was born in 1860, and grew up in this house with three sisters and two brothers. A 45-minute guided tour provides an entertaining glimpse of Gordon family life.

The house was completed in 1821 for then-Mayor of Savannah, James Moore Wayne, who sold the house 10 years later to his niece Sarah and her husband, William Washington Gordon. It originally had two stories over a basement floor. The third floor was added in 1886 to accommodate a large family. Also in 1886, damage from an earthquake necessitated major interior changes to the house, and the interpretation of the house today is based on the 1886 period.

There are many furnishings that were Gordon pieces and a surprising number of art works created by Daisy herself. The library contains some of her sculptures as well as a carved piece of furniture. She was a painter also, on canvas and on porcelain, and several of these works are displayed in the house. One of her paintings is a copy of a portrait of Nellie Kinzie Gordon. Daisy had an eye for art, and the paintings in the entry hall were known to be her favorites.

The rooms of the house are large and feature elaborate decorative details. Intricately carved crown moldings and massive crystal chandeliers bespeak an age of elegance. Portraits of family members and others help tell the story of the Gordon family and the period in which they lived. Upstairs, the bedrooms are furnished with family pieces, and one room contains furniture that belonged to Juliette Low. On display are two dollhouses, sure to delight the younger set. One of these is a rare Georgia Plains style farmhouse, intact with its hinged front-piece. Visitors will learn about the research for the wall colors and about the use of wallpapers in houses of this period.

The garden on the side of the house is particularly appealing in the spring when many plants and shrubs are in bloom. From the garden, visitors can obtain a good view of the piazza which was added in 1886 when other major renovations were underway.

Juliette Gordon Low founded the Girl Scouts in 1912. Her birthplace was purchased and restored by the Girl Scouts of the USA in 1953. It was designated a National Historic Landmark in 1965. Each year thousands of Girl Scouts from all over America visit the birthplace of their founder and learn about the legacy of the Gordon family.

ACROSS

1. In 1886 a _____ floor was added to Juliette's house
3. Juliette was a talented _____
4. Juliette's last name after she married
5. Important 1886 event for the Gordon family
9. Organization founded in 1912 by Juliette
10. One of the streets bordering this house
11. This house and its history are part of Savannah's _____

DOWN

1. This house has _____ stories over a basement
2. Juliette's initials
6. Juliette may have played with a _____ such as those upstairs
7. Juliette's nickname
8. An earth_____ caused much damage to this house
9. Juliette's maiden name

ANSWER KEY:

ACROSS
1. third
3. artist
4. Low
5. wedding
9. Girl Scouts
10. Bull
11. heritage

DOWN
1. three
2. JGL
6. dollhouse
7. Daisy
8. quake
9. Gordon

14

KING-TISDELL COTTAGE

514 East Huntington Street
Savannah, GA 31401
(912) 234-8000
www.kingtisdell.org

DAYS/HOURS OF OPERATION
These vary; please call to verify

ADMISSION
$3 per adult
$2 per student

FACILITIES
Parking
Restrooms

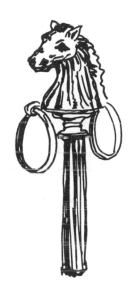

HINTS
* Allow 30 minutes
* Combine with visit to Beach Institute nearby

"I wish I could live in this house."

Katie Ratterree, age 4

This charming Victorian house was built in 1896 as rental property and was restored meticulously in the 1980s prior to opening as a museum. Arriving at the house, visitors are drawn to the intricate ornamentation, or "gingerbread," that decorates the exterior. The gingerbread trim found here is unusually detailed for a house of this modest size. For children, the cottage seems to have been plucked right out of a storybook!

Tours begin on the front porch, a reminder of the days when street life was lively and neighbors spent time on their porches. The house was built for Mr. W. W. Aimar, who sold it to Mr. and Mrs. Eugene King in 1910. Following Mr. King's death, Mrs. King married Mr. Robert Tisdell, hence the name of the cottage. Collections include art objects and historical documents relating to slavery. Among the items displayed are shackles and recorded deeds of the sale of slaves, and photos, tintypes and other items from the Willis Jones Collection of Slavery Memorabilia.

The fenced garden in the rear of the cottage features the slave well-house removed from historic Wormsloe Plantation.

LIVE OAK PUBLIC LIBRARIES

Main branch: 2002 Bull Street
Savannah, GA 31401
912 652-3630
www.liveoakpl.org

- -

DAYS/HOURS OF OPERATION
Main branch, Monday through Thursday: 9 a.m. to 9 p.m.
Friday and Saturday: 9 a.m. to 6 p.m.
Sunday: 2 p.m. to 6 p.m.

Hours vary for other branches

ADMISSION
Free

FACILITIES
Book lending via Library card system
    (free for residents of Chatham,
    Effingham and Liberty Counties)
Computers with internet access
Free wireless internet at many branches
Handicapped accessible
Offstreet parking (limited)
Reference room
Restrooms
Water fountains

SPECIAL PROGRAMS
Savannah Children's Book Festival (November)
Vacation Reading Program (Summer)
Winter Reading Program (December-January)
Partner with Read It Loud! Savannah and The Big Read-Savannah

HINTS
* Allow one hour
* Combine with a picnic or lunch outing

"I like to do art projects at the library."

Carey Bass, age 3

"I like it when Mrs. Sha (head children's librarian) reads stories."

Langston Bass, age 3

Live Oak Public Libraries has 19 branches in Chatham, Effingham and Liberty Counties (listed on page 19) and one coming soon in southwest Chatham. Most branches offer activities for children and are located throughout the three counties - there is surely one close to your neighborhood. For those who cannot visit a branch, games and interactive materials are available online.

A library adventure entertains children while also giving moms and caretakers a change of scenery. Literary and creative activities will introduce young minds to the worlds that await in books and stories. Children from toddlers (known as "Tree Tots" at Live Oak) to preschoolers ("Acorns") will enjoy story-telling, crafts, games and other age-appropriate activities. Even infants are welcome for storytime! Older children (ages 8 to 16) will enjoy their own programs, which feature crafts, games, creative writing, karaoke, poetry and art.

Occasionally there are special programs such as puppet shows and other performing arts. Be sure and ask for information or check the website regularly for upcoming events.

Regular visits to the children's activity sessions can be followed by selecting and checking out books to enjoy at home. The hours of programs vary at each branch, but range from morning to after school. Visiting different branches is a fun way to change the routine and meet new faces. The branch buildings vary in style and size, and the locations make visits convenient for just about anyone. Combining a visit with lunch and/or a playground picnic enriches the adventure.

A favorite Savannah event for children of all ages is the Savannah Children's Book Festival, which takes place in the fall. Forsyth Park is transformed into a book wonderland, featuring children's book authors and illustrators from around the country, musical performers, arts and crafts, and costumed characters. Each summer, thousands of area children and teens sign up for the popular Vacation Reading Program, tracking their reading hours for fun and prizes and enjoying special programs at every branch.

The website has several links on the Kids page to interactive games for all ages. School-aged children will find research links to GALILEO, the State's Digital Library, Biography Resource Center and FactMonster. The website also posts School Reading Lists for all elementary and some middle schools and now links these lists directly to the Library's catalog (making it much easier for parents, teachers and students to find their books).

Branches are listed by name here, and addresses and directions to each can be found on the website or by calling the main branch.

Chatham County: Bull Street, Carnegie, Hitch, Kayton, Ogeechee, Ola Wyeth, W. W. Law, Islands, Thunderbolt, Tybee, Oglethorpe Mall, Forest City, Port City (Garden City), Port Wentworth, West Chatham (Pooler), Southwest Chatham (underway).

Effingham County: Effingham, South Effingham (Rincon)

Liberty County: Liberty (Hinesville), Midway/Riceboro

MASSIE HERITAGE CENTER: SAVANNAH'S TEACHING MUSEUM FOR HISTORY AND ARCHITECTURE- WHERE HISTORY COMES ALIVE!

207 East Gordon Street
Savannah, GA 31401
(912) 201-5070
www.massieschool.com

DAYS/HOURS OF OPERATION
Monday-Friday: 9 a.m. - 4 p.m.

ADMISSION
Self-Guided $3
Guided Tour $5 (call ahead to schedule)
Children under 4, free

FACILITIES
Gardens
Gift Shop
Restrooms
Soda Machine

SPECIAL EVENTS
May Day Celebration
Georgia Heritage Celebration
"Breaking the Bonds" tour

"That giant eye from an old building is spooky.
I like all the fancy decorations that some of the
downtown houses have."

Katie Ratterree, age 5

Where might one find the Parthenon in Savannah? How about the Cathedral of Notre Dame? A remnant of a Roman aqueduct? The house that Rhett Butler built for Scarlett after the Civil War? Or the gingerbread house from the tale of Hansel and Gretel?

They are all here, and the teaching installations at Massie will show where to find them. In a city which holds its town plan and significant architecture in high regard, Massie should be the first stop for anyone who wants to understand the origins of Savannah's built environment. Children will enjoy the museum scavenger hunt and hands-on activities in each teaching installation.

Massie is owned and operated by the local public school system as a teaching museum. It was built as a school and is known locally as Massie School. Greek Revival in style, the center building was designed by the New York architect John Norris who had been hired to design the U.S. Customs House on Bay Street. The two annexes, connected to Norris' building by catwalks, were added later. The school is named for Peter Massie, whose will, dated 1841, provided for the construction of a school for poor children. The school opened in October, 1856.

Visitors will enjoy the exceptional exhibits which tie Savannah's many architectural styles to classical, European, and even modern architecture. While guided tours are available, most visitors choose a self-guided tour. The displays are well-labeled and easy to follow. The western annex, a good place to begin, houses an exhibit showing the city plan that guided Savannah's development for over a century. The scale model of the historic district in the center of the room is the only three-dimensional model of the city. Children will enjoy searching for streets, museums or squares they might have passed or plan to visit.

Next stop should be the center building's main floor exhibit, which depicts the classic revival styles that predominated in Savannah's architecture during the nineteenth century. The eastern annex contains the Victorian Era exhibit. Especially appealing during the Victorian era is the abundance of decoration applied to buildings. Whether made of wood, brick or terracotta, buildings from this Victorian period come alive through their fanciful ornamentation. Looking for these details while touring the city makes for a lively treasure hunt. A new exhibit in this installation features W.W. Law, a well-known Savannah Civil Rights leader and historic preservationist.

Two exhibits are located upstairs, reached by two staircases: one for boys, one for girls. The east wing features an exhibit of Native Americans in Coastal Georgia.

Also upstairs is the Heritage Classroom, a nineteenth century classroom in which children may participate in school activities like those long ago. Write on a slateboard or perform oral recitation while sitting up straight in the desk. Most children leave this room with newfound appreciation for today's classroom!

NEGRO HERITAGE TRAIL TOUR: AN AFRICAN-AMERICAN JOURNEY

502 East Harris Street
Savannah, GA 31401
(912) 234-8000
Tour departs from the Savannah Visitor Information Center,
   301 Martin Luther King Blvd.
www.kingtisdell.org

■ ■

DAYS/HOURS OF OPERATION
10 a.m. and 12 noon

ADMISSION
$19 per adult, $10 per child ages 10 to 16, free for children under 10
Group discounts and step-on tours are available

HINTS
* Allow two and a half hours
* Revisit sites pointed out along the way

> *"I like the places we stopped. We heard about
> the Underground Railroad, and I had learned
> about that in school."*
>
> *Joe Ratterree, age 9*

The Negro Heritage Trail Tour, founded by Savannah Civil Rights leader W. W. Law, is a two-hour guided bus tour that presents Savannah's African-American history. The tour stops at several significant sites: First African Baptist Church, King-Tisdell Cottage, and the Beach Institute African-American Cultural Arts Center. Leaving from the Visitors Center, the tour winds through the National Historic Landmark District and includes a section of the riverfront and Laurel Grove Cemetery. Entertaining for all ages, this tour presents many little-known facts about the African-American heritage in Savannah and its role in the rice and cotton industries. The tour also provides details about the African-American participation in the Revolutionary and Civil Wars. Visitors learn about the advent of

slavery in Savannah and may hear for the first time that freedom could be purchased long before abolition. A tour through Laurel Grove Cemetery reveals the burial sites of such prominent citizens as Andrew Cox Marshall and Andrew Bryant, both preachers in Savannah.

The importance of the church in the African-American community begins with the First African Baptist Church, founded in 1773, as the oldest African-American congregation in North America. After almost a century of worshipping in various locations throughout Savannah, the congregation built the current sanctuary in 1859 of brick, later covered with stucco. Of particular interest are the African markings on the upper balcony pews. These are examples of an art form called marbleizing and depict the signatures of those who built the pews. On the main floor, the diamond-shaped patterns cut into the floor represent an African religious symbol, and they also provided ventilation for escaped slaves hidden beneath the building. Special Field Order 15, the document which promised "forty acres and a mule" to newly freed African-Americans, was drafted by General William T. Sherman in the Green-Meldrim House just a few blocks southeast of this church, and proclaimed publicly at the historic Second African Baptist Church.

Two other stops on the tour, the King-Tisdell Cottage and the Beach Institute African-American Cultural Arts Center, are covered elsewhere in this book. The stops made during the tour make for a comfortable two hours with children.

THE PIRATES' HOUSE

20 East Broad Street
Savannah, GA 31401
(912) 233-5757
www.thepirateshouse.com

DAYS/HOURS OF OPERATION
7 days per week
Lunch: 11:30 a.m. - 3 p.m.
Afternoon desserts, coffee: 3 p.m. - 5 p.m. daily
Dinner: 5 p.m. - 9 p.m.

COST
Children's Menu with items ranging from $2 to $7.25
Special drinks for children

FACILITIES
Brochures
Gift shop
Handicapped access
Parking
Restrooms
Restaurant

HINTS
* Come early for lunch or dinner with children
* Birthday Parties and Special Events welcomed
* Allow 1½ to 2 hours
* Plan to have dessert

"I like the pirate with the gun in his boot the best, the one named Long John Silver. I like the sign that's hanging that has a sword. I like the dungeon. The fish on the menu is my favorite. I like the pirate that talks when you push the button. And I like Blackbeard's Boot with the fruit drink and the parakeets in the bird cage."

Billy McKee, age 4

The Pirates' House has been a landmark in Savannah since 1753. Although now it functions exclusively as a restaurant with unique charm for children, it is recognized by the American Museum Society as an authentic house museum.

Originally The Pirates' House operated as an inn for seafarers and subsequently became a hang-out for pirates and sailors from Singapore to Bombay and from London to Port Said. Visitors enter the restaurant through heavy wooden doors into a dimly-lit interior. The maitre d' greets young guests with a pirate's hat which doubles as the children's menu. Seafaring pictures and paraphernalia ornament the walls and give the maze of rooms an authentic aura.

While waiting for a meal, young visitors will want to seek out the life-sized, robotized pirate who talks and moves when children push a button on the wall. Sometimes called Captain Flint, the pirate tells jokes and stories. Another life-sized pirate, Jolly George, is placed at the top of a winding stone staircase which leads to the wine cellar, or possibly to a secret tunnel. Legend has it that sailors were shanghaied through this tunnel to the nearby Savannah River at night and brought aboard anchored ships which set sail before the hapless sailors awoke.

Older children may be inspired to read Robert Louis Stevenson's *Treasure Island*, which contains numerous references to Savannah. Indeed, Old Captain Flint may have died in an upstairs room of The Pirates' House, and some say his ghost still haunts the building.

The Pirates' House operates 15 separate dining rooms, each unique. Two of these are situated in the "Herb House," said to have been erected in 1734 and possibly the oldest building in Georgia.

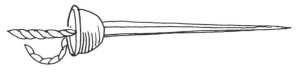

RALPH MARK GILBERT
CIVIL RIGHTS MUSEUM

460 Martin Luther King, Jr. Boulevard
Savannah, GA 31401
912-231-8900
www.sip.armstrong.edu/CivilRightsMuseum/Civilindex

DAYS/HOURS OF OPERATION
Monday - Saturday: 9 a.m. to 5 p.m.

ADMISSION
$4 per adult
   $3 for groups of 10 or more
$2 per student
$3 per senior citizen

FACILITIES
Free parking off street
Gift shop
Handicapped accessible
Restrooms
Special programs for children,
   including a Youth Activity Guide
Video presentation
Water fountain

HINTS
* Consider combining with a visit to another downtown site
* Allow one hour for a visit

"Sam Gillian is an artist and he did this art - towel with
different shapes, squares, triangles and circles.
It was awesome. There was also a big cloth with lots of
colors thrown on with two paint brushes.
It was a fun place to visit."

Ke'ambra Pinckney, age 10

"I like the way they show the movie in a room that looks like a church."

Joe Ratterree, age 12

This museum tells the story of Civil Rights in Savannah through a pictorial timeline, memorabilia, exhibits and a video presentation. Established in 1998, the museum is named for Dr. Ralph Mark Gilbert, an orator, playwright, preacher and leader of the Savannah Branch of the NAACP who is recognized as the father of Savannah's Civil Rights movement. The museum is located on Martin Luther King, Jr. Blvd. in a 1914 building that housed the black-owned Wage Earners Savings and Loan Bank. The street, formerly known as West Broad Street, is prominent in the history of Savannah and its African -American citizens.

The exhibit's large photographs and artifacts are organized to depict segregation in both the public sector, such as hospitals, housing and buses, and the private sector, such as lunch counters, stores, water fountains and restrooms. Etched into granite panels are phrases which seem unreal today, but which were part of the day-to-day existence in the 1940s, '50s and '60s: "White applicants only," "Negro entrance at rear" and "Colored dining room in rear." Young visitors will learn about the boycott of local businesses and merchants by the black community and about the role of students in the organized lunch counter sit-ins in downtown Savannah.

Special sections of the exhibit depict segregation in schools, in Savannah's political life and on Broughton Street, where many stores and restaurants were located. There is also an exhibit of a downtown lunch counter during a sit-in, when African-Americans were admitted entry but were not served a meal.

An 18-minute video in an upstairs gallery chronicles the local history of civil rights through interviews with African-Americans who played important roles during this time. The film is shown in a room that resembles a church, with pews and stained glass windows. Many important meetings during the civil rights movement were held in black churches, centers of the African-American community in Savannah.

Tours are self guided unless arrangements have been made for a group. There are other exhibits here relating to the history of African-Americans in Savannah. A Tour Activity Guide is available that will keep children focused and also will serve as a reminder of their visit.

RIVER STREET AND BAY STREET

"When big cargo ships come up the river, they seem so close you could reach out and touch them!"

Joe Ratterree, age 9

"I like to chase the seagulls on the sidewalk, and play in the tugboat sandbox."

Katie Ratterree, age 4

River Street, Savannah's northern boundary, has been a part of Savannah's history since James Edward Oglethorpe landed here in 1733 to establish the colony of Georgia at Savannah. The street today is far different from the rugged bluff glimpsed by the first settlers.

Rising up from the cobblestone street are tall buildings four and five stories high. The sides of the buildings which face Bay Street are only two stories high. During the 19th century, when cotton was king, the upper stories were used for conducting the business of cotton trading while the lower stories on the River Street side were used to warehouse the cotton. The walkways spanned by narrow pedestrian bridges are called Factors' Walk, referring to the business of factoring and trading that went on inside the buildings.

Cotton was a major business for the port of Savannah, creating jobs and wealth for many. River Street was a center of this activity. The stones paving River Street, called cobblestones or ballast stones, were used as ballast on empty ships entering Savannah from Europe and were left behind to make room aboard for cotton headed out of port. A striking reminder of the era is the red brick and terra cotta Cotton Exchange building, between the Bull and Abercorn Street ramps.

Like much of the downtown area, River Street was largely abandoned during the early part of the twentieth century. However, the preservation effort, begun downtown in the 1950s, gained momentum, and River Street was restored in 1976 by the City of Savannah as a bicentennial project.

Walkways, balustrades, landscaping and seating brought River Street back to life. Today there is a variety of restaurants, shops, museums, and activities. Browsing, eating, shopping, exploring, walking and watching for big ships are just a few of the adventures that could fill several hours of time. A paddlewheel boat awaits boarding for a harbor cruise and ferries are available to take passengers across the river and back.

There are sidewalks along the buildings and storefronts and wide brick walkways closer to the river. For very young children who need to work off steam, there is a sandbox area with a small-fry tugboat in its center. The Waving Girl statue on the eastern end of the street commemorates Florence Martus, who from the 1880s to the 1930s is said to have greeted every ship entering or leaving the port by waving a white cloth during the day and a lantern at night. Often a huge container ship will pass by, stirring a vision of stowaways and travels to far off places and leaving even grown-ups agog at the size of the vessels.

Few children (or parents, for that matter) will be able to resist exploring the ramps and stone stairways that lead up to the Bay Street level. There are as many landmarks and sights of interest here as there are down below on River Street. From City Hall, with its distinctive gold dome, east toward the beautiful live-oak shaded Emmet Park, there are fountains, cannons, lions, bells, and monuments worth investigating. Visitors can get back to River Street by walking down the cobblestone streets or stone stairways from Factors' Walk.

ROUNDHOUSE RAILROAD MUSEUM

Managed by the Coastal Heritage Society
601 West Harris Street
Savannah, GA 31401
(912) 651-6823
www.chsgeorgia.org

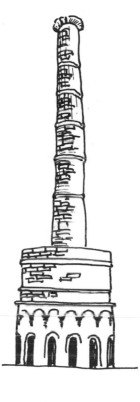

DAYS/HOURS OF OPERATION
Daily: 9 a.m. - 5 p.m.
(Closed Thanksgiving, Christmas, New Years Day)
Self-guided tours all day

ADMISSION
$4.25 per adult
$3.75 per child 6-11, and senior citizens

FACILITIES
Food/Drink machine
Gift Shop
Handicapped access
Museum
Parking
Picnic area
Restrooms

HINTS
* Be sure to visit the Kidz Zone
* Allow an hour
* Parties welcome. Birthday parties in the caboose are popular.
  Special tours can include operation of locomotive turntable and
  model train.
* Call for information

"My favorite thing was the turntable and what was
interesting was the machines we got to see."

Billy McKee, age 5

The Roundhouse Railroad Museum comprises the antebellum Roundhouse Complex and Historic Railroad Shops, a National Historic Landmark. Take a fascinating step into the golden era of trains and the flowering of the industrial revolution in Savannah. This five-acre site, owned by the City of Savannah and opened to the public in 1991, hosts 11 buildings constructed in 1855 and 1926 for the servicing of trains and their engines. In fact, this site contains the oldest and most complete railroad repair shops in the United States.

For train enthusiasts and others this site is a real treat, for there is a restored, operating turntable here, one of the few operating turntables in the country. The electric turntable, located in the center of the site, allowed locomotives to enter or exit a maintenance stall in the Roundhouse. It is an ingenious device, replacing the original which was turned by hand in the mid-1800s. It serviced approximately 36 tracks to facilitate the repair and maintenance of locomotives.

Also located at the Roundhouse Railroad Museum is a series of buildings which served as the "overhaul" or back shop, the carpentry shop, the blacksmith shop, the machine shop, the storehouse, and the tender frame shop. Visitors will see a 1914 steam locomotive, antique machinery, the oldest portable steam engine in the country, and hundreds of other railroad artifacts.

There is an impressive 125-foot-tall brick smokestack built in 1853 to draw smoke from the nearby Blacksmith Shop and the Boiler/Engine Shop through underground ducts. The Tender Frame Shop, which is air-conditioned, houses exhibits of tools from various shops utilized in maintaining and repairing locomotives and tools used for laying track.

This unusual site, originally built and operated by the Central of Georgia Railway, at one time operated as one of the South's premier repair facilities. Chartered in 1833 as the Central Railroad and Canal Company, it was formed to prevent the diversion of the cotton shipping trade to Charleston.

Visitors enter through the Museum Shop, housed in the old Dispatch Office. The shop is full of items related to railroading and Georgia history. The site also features an 18-minute film, *Steam, Steel and Sweat: The Story of Savannah's Railroad Shops*, that provides a history of and orientation to the site. Future plans call for the development of an excursion train program at the site.

SAVANNAH HISTORY MUSEUM

Managed by The Coastal Heritage Society
303 Martin Luther King Jr. Blvd.
Savannah, GA 31401
(912) 651-6825
www.chsgeorgia.org

DAYS/HOURS OF OPERATION
Weekdays: 8:30 a.m. - 5 p.m.
Weekends: 9 a.m. - 5 p.m.
Closed Thanksgiving, Christmas, New Years Day

ADMISSION
$4.25 per adult
$3.75 per child 6-11 and senior citizens,
Children under 6, free

FACILITIES
Full Service Deli and Restaurant
Gift Shop
Handicapped access
Parking
Restrooms
Visitors Center

HINTS
* Allow an hour
* Check on movie show times
* Special parties catered. Call for information

"My favorite part of the museum was seeing
the big cannon in the museum and buying a
small cannon in the Gift Shop."

Billy McKee, age 5

What was once a bustling passenger depot for the Central of Georgia Railway is now the Savannah History Museum. The Museum opened in 1990 to preserve and display Savannah's cultural and historic heritage. Many visitors to Savannah make this their first stop because of its location in the Savannah Visitor Information Center.

The Savannah History Museum building dates from 1860, when it operated to serve the railroad. That function ended in 1971. In 1977, the old depot was designated a National Historic Landmark. But even before the railroad depot was built, this site was the location of a major Revolutionary War battle.

On October 9, 1779, over 7000 men from three continents (Europe, North America, and Africa) fought for possession of Savannah. Here American and French soldiers fought British soldiers in a bloody battle that left more than 800 men wounded or dead. At the Battle of Spring Hill, the American and French soldiers suffered a crushing defeat at the hand of the British. Using lead soldiers, local historian Preston Russell has recreated the battle scene inside the museum.

Children will enjoy seeing a real steam locomotive built in 1890 for the Central of Georgia Railroad. Other exhibits include Civil War artifacts, Native-American artifacts, soldiers' uniforms, maps and prints of Old Savannah, river and sea exhibits, a cotton gin, real bales of cotton, and an impressive collection of documents on Georgia's African-American military history. Stacks of cannon balls and artillery projectiles will attract younger children. These Confederate projectiles were recovered from the *CSS Georgia*, a floating battery built in 1862 to defend the Savannah River from the advance of General Sherman's troops. Confederate soldiers sank the *CSS Georgia* to prevent Union troops from capturing the battery, and the ship still rests on the bottom of the Savannah River near Fort Jackson.

This site also has a full-service restaurant, The Whistle Stop Café.

SAVANNAH NATIONAL WILDLIFE REFUGE

Owned and managed by U.S. Fish and Wildlife Service
1000 Business Center Drive
Parkway Business Center, Suite 10
Savannah, GA 31405
(912) 652-4415
Refuge Location.
Entrance to Laurel Hill Wildlife Drive, on S.C. Highway 170,
  north of the Houlihan Bridge
www.fws.gov/savannah/

- -

DAYS/HOURS OF OPERATION
Daylight only

ADMISSION
Free

FACILITIES
Parking
Restrooms
Trails

HINTS
* Bug spray is a must during warm weather
* Do not bring pets
* Stay on cleared dikes and paths
* Bring binoculars

"We liked seeing the owl on her nest, but we didn't get
too close, and we liked seeing the alligators."

Mary Ellen McKee, age 13; Tom McKee, age 10; Billy McKee, age 5

The Savannah National Wildlife Refuge is a short drive from downtown Savannah, straddling the border of Georgia and South Carolina. For nature enthusiasts, this is a delightful respite from the urban environment. Birds and alligators are abundant in the refuge, which covers 29,175 acres of freshwater marsh, tidal rivers and creeks, and bottomland hardwood swamps.

This wildlife refuge was established in 1927, encompassing as many as 13 former rice plantations. The 3000 acres of freshwater impoundments are maintained in the same manner as they were when rice was grown in the late 18th and 19th centuries. "Trunks" or flood-gates allow water from the Savannah River to enter at high tide or exit at low tide. Tidal power and trunks made of treated pine offer the most efficient method of controlling water levels in the refuge, even in the twenty-first century.

The best way to see the refuge is to begin at the main entrance and follow the four-mile Laurel Hill Drive around the eastern part of the refuge. This driving tour is a quick way for children to see the refuge, with stops for short hikes or picnicking. There is lots to see from the car, particularly in fall, winter, and spring. A pair of bald eagles frequents the refuge in late winter, and great horned owls have become refuge mascots because of a favorite nesting spot right at the beginning of Laurel Hill Drive.

Wonderful live oak trees border the small rise at the entrance of the refuge, which once was the Laurel Hill Plantation home site. The only restrooms in the refuge area are at this entrance (portable toilets).

Laurel Hill Drive wanders along earthen dikes built two centuries ago which separate the freshwater impoundments. On the right of the drive is the Savannah River and the very visible signs of Savannah's major industries. Driving further, this urban view is obscured by forest, and visitors are surrounded by the sights and sounds of the refuge.

Wading birds, shorebirds, waterfowl, hawks, owls, the rare swallow-tailed kite, the bald eagle, and even the peregrine falcon are possible sightings among 260 species of birds that regularly visit the refuge. Alligators, turtles, otters, snakes, or a mink might be seen in the water or on the banks of the ponds and creeks. Deer, raccoons, bobcats, and opossums are also residents here, although they are very shy and usually difficult to spot.

Guided tours are available with advance arrangements. Because of limited Fish and Wildlife staff, volunteers regularly lead tours through the refuge, hiking Cistern Trail and pointing out difficult-to-see wildlife. Fishing is permitted from March 1 through November 30 within the impoundment system (dike enclosed pools). Bank fishing from the wildlife drive is permitted year round. A South Carolina fishing license is required to fish from the drive or within the impoundments. Limited hunting seasons in October, November, and March are permitted, and during these times certain areas of the refuge are off-limits to visitors. Restrictions are also placed on the area north of U.S. Highway 17 to protect wintering waterfowl from December 1 to February 28. Parts of the refuge are accessible only by boat or on foot. There are 25 miles of dikes for hardy hikers or bikers, but this is not recommended for young children.

The refuge is not only a haven for wildlife, but also a retreat for people who will enjoy glimpsing life on the undeveloped side of the Savannah River.

WORD SEARCH

```
C D X S U P Q A N F Z O L M Y X O
B E T F Z A M Y L P C N D F J G T
G A C H J I K O Q R T Y F T V S T
Z G O L M Z A L L I G A T O R Z E
D L K N Q O R B S P X R A W K B R
D E E R A T N I K B E H J L N Q Z
J B Q M Z Y S T C D N O K M F F N
A Z S L F D B K O E J B S N A K E
N T I D E S C F H I L O P R L Q B
Z T U N B O P Q C F D B G J C H X
X L M R Z C E G O D U C K I O L P
A Z B Y T D X C V L T A M U N Z V
V N U S R L K A D B Z T X C R P T
R P Z D H G E K U N V S W A M P O
```

TIDE	ALLIGATOR	RICE	OTTER
SNAKE	DEER	FALCON	
EAGLE	OWL	TURTLE	
BOBCAT	DUCK	SWAMP	

SAVANNAH'S SQUARES AND FORSYTH PARK

"We always have an adventure when we go downtown. Every square has something different."

Joe Ratterree, age 8

"My favorite place is the big playground at Forsyth Park. The slides there are very tall. I also like the square by the college, where I like to get something to eat and drink."

Katie Ratterree, age 5

A walk through Savannah's historic district is a walk back in time. Whether strolling along the bluff overlooking the Savannah River or resting on a park bench under the canopy of centuries-old oaks, visitors will fall captive to the relaxed pace of an earlier time. Savannah's original town plan, brought by founder James Edward Oglethorpe in 1733, defines the pace. The crown jewels of the town plan are Savannah's squares, oases of calm in the fast lane of city life. Of the 24 squares that were laid out between 1733 and 1856, 22 exist today, imposing a sense of order and harmony within the 2.2 square mile historic district. Around the squares there are shops, classroom buildings, homes, museums, restaurants, churches and businesses in restored nineteenth century buildings that narrowly escaped demolition during the 1940s and 1950s.

A key to understanding the town plan is to remember the function of the squares as gathering places for the surrounding homes and businesses. In the 18th century, fear of attack from any number of enemies was very real, and the squares were places where colonists could gather for protection. They were also used to corral animals. The four large lots facing east and west on each square, called trust lots, were reserved for buildings of prominence, such as churches, civic buildings, and later for residences of prominent citizens.

The four lots on the north and south sides of each square were called tything lots, because they were each divided into 10 lots intended for homes. Therefore, each square was the center of a neighborhood called a ward, and the entire system of wards and squares was continued until 1851.

There are several tour companies in Savannah that give a complete story of Savannah's history, architecture and preservation movement. The Massie Heritage Center, housed in the Massie School building on Calhoun Square, provides a fine overview of the Historic District.

The Savannah College of Art and Design (SCAD) has a significant presence in the downtown area. Established in 1978 in the National Guard Armory Building on Madison Square, SCAD today occupies several buildings in the Historic and Victorian Districts. The presence of students adds vitality to the area.

The following paragraphs describe a few squares that have special appeal for children. All of the squares have shade and benches, and most are visited by peanut-loving pigeons and squirrels. A bag of nuts may allow a new friendship to blossom!

JOHNSON SQUARE, the first square laid out in 1733, is downtown Savannah's financial center and keeps a lively pace. It is named for South Carolina colonial Governor Robert Johnson. Located here is Christ Church, the first church in Georgia. On certain days of the week, musical performances take place in the square around lunchtime, drawing a wide array of people to hear everything from jazz to string quartets. Cart vendors offer fast food a la historic district; traditional fast food restaurants are hard to find here. In the center of Johnson Square is a monument to Nathanael Greene, who served as Chief of Staff to George Washington in the American Revolution, and who was given Mulberry Grove Plantation near Savannah in appreciation for his military service. There are two fountains in this square, where wishes can be made with the toss of a coin.

WRIGHT SQUARE, at one time called Court House Square, is home to two major government buildings, the Federal Building and the Chatham County Courthouse. It is named for Sir James Wright, the last Royal Governor of Georgia. In its center is a monument to William Washington Gordon who was Mayor of Savannah and the grandfather of

Juliette Gordon Low, founder of the Girl Scouts. In one corner of the square is a large granite boulder which was placed to honor Yamacraw Indian Chief Tomochichi, whose friendship was invaluable to Oglethorpe in settling the colony. Local tradition holds that if one walks around the boulder three times, knocks on it, and asks Tomochichi what he is doing, he'll say nothing!

CHIPPEWA SQUARE features in its center a statue of General James Edward Oglethorpe, founder of the colony of Georgia at Savannah on February 12, 1733. The statute was created by artist Daniel Chester French. It is said that Oglethorpe faces south because that is the direction from which the colonial enemy, the Spanish forces in Florida, would have come.

MADISON SQUARE is probably Savannah's most diverse with homes, a church, a hotel, several shops, a college, and the Green-Meldrim House, which served as headquarters for General Sherman during the Union occupation of Savannah. There is always a high level of activity here. In the center is a statue of Revolutionary War hero Sergeant William Jasper, commander of Fort Moultrie who was killed in the attack on Savannah, October 9, 1779. The statue shows Jasper rescuing his company's flag. On the southern end of the square are two cannons which are irresistible for climbing and unbeatable for photo opportunities.

MONTEREY SQUARE features Savannah's finest assortment of ornamental ironwork. Just about every shape, size and configuration can be found on the balconies and high stoops of the homes on this square. The pelican newel posts at 4 West Taylor are of great interest to children. Guarding the entry to the house, each pelican holds in its raised claw a pebble, which, if the pelican fell asleep, would fall to the ground, making a noise that would wake the pelican to resume its sentinel duties. Pencils, crayons and paper may come in handy to draw some of the patterns found the ironwork.

FORSYTH PARK, laid out in 1851 and named for Governor John Forsyth, is a favorite for walkers and joggers. The cast iron fountain in its center, erected in 1858, is surrounded by bricks engraved with names of those who assisted in the restoration of the fountain in 1988. The northern section of the park is like a giant maze. Sidewalks wind through landscaped sections planted with azaleas and many species of trees and shrubbery. The playground space located in the middle of the park is a favorite for children. The two structures near the playgrounds were built after World War I as dummy forts for military training. One of these was converted into a fragrant

garden for the blind. In the southern section of the park are expanses of grass used as playing fields and for outdoor performance seating. Along the central axis are two statues, one a monument in sandstone honoring the Confederate dead, and the other a bronze statue commemorating those who served in the Spanish-American War. Tennis and basketball courts are located at this end of the park. Forsyth Park is a favorite place for festivals and celebrations.

Across Drayton Street from Forsyth Park is the **CANDLER OAK**, the largest live oak tree in the Historic District, estimated to be between 200 and 300 years old. This tree is protected by a conservation easement held by the Savannah Tree Foundation.

COLONIAL CEMETERY is located at the intersection of Abercorn Street and Oglethorpe Avenue. In earlier centuries it served as a burial ground for both the parish of Christ Church and the city. At the end of its use as a cemetery, its maintenance was turned over to the Park and Tree Commission. Today it is enjoyed as a passive park. There are some lovely old gravestones here, and markers identify well-known names in Savannah's and Georgia's history. At the southern end of the cemetery is a playground. Across Abercorn Street is a rather large fire station in an older building. Most young children enjoy seeing the enormous trucks, and the local firemen enjoy showing them around. Consider exploring other historic city-owned cemeteries, Bonaventure and Laurel Grove. For more information call 651-6043.

SAVANNAH VISITOR INFORMATION CENTER

301 Martin Luther King, Jr. Blvd.
Savannah, GA 31401
(912) 944-0455
www.savcvb.com

DAYS/HOURS OF OPERATION
Monday-Friday: 8:30 a.m. - 5 p.m.
Saturday and Sunday: 9 a.m. - 5 p.m.
Holidays: 9 a.m. - 5 p.m.
Closed Thanksgiving, Christmas, New Years Day

ADMISSION
Free

FACILITIES
Gift Shop
Information
Parking
Restrooms

HINTS
* Begin Savannah visit here
* Combine with visits to nearby Roundhouse Railroad Museum and
  Savannah History Museum

"I like the snack bar."

Billy McKee, age 5

The Savannah Visitor Information Center, managed by the Savannah Area
Convention & Visitors Bureau, is located in the restored passenger depot of the
Central of Georgia Railway, built in 1860. Sharing the building with the
Savannah History Museum, the Center is a great place for the newcomer in

Savannah to begin. Staffed with personnel willing to offer assistance, the Visitor Information Center has racks of brochures, complimentary maps, and a courtesy phone for reservations at Bed and Breakfast Inn, tour companies, hotels and motels. It is also the originating point for all trolley or bus tours.

The enclosed atrium, located between the Visitor Information Center and the Savannah History Museum, offers tables and chairs and access to refreshments at the snack bar. Located in the atrium are large, painted murals depicting Savannah's founders and influential citizens, historic scenes, and a model of the Great Savannah Exposition in 1985.

The Center provides a general orientation to Savannah with generous parking facilities. A little pre-planning here will help visitors make the most of their time.

SHIPS OF THE SEA MUSEUM

41 Martin Luther King, Jr. Blvd.
Savannah, GA 31401
(912) 232-1511
www.shipsofthesea.org

- -

DAYS/HOURS OF OPERATION
Tuesday through Sunday: 10 a.m. to 5 p.m.

ADMISSION
$8 per adult
$6 per senior citizen, AAA, military, students
$20 for family rate
Children 6 and under, free

FACILITIES
Garden
Gift Shop
Parking Lot
Restrooms

HINTS
* Group tours and activities with reservations

> "The ships are remarkable. I liked the ships in the bottle.
> There was a cannon too."
>
> *Tom McKee, Jr., age 9*

There are many reasons to visit the Ships of the Sea Museum. Children will be fascinated by the maritime history chronicled through large models of ships recalling seafaring adventures of earlier centuries. The museum is housed in an 1819 mansion built for William Scarbrough, a financier of the *Savannah*, the first steamship to cross the Atlantic Ocean. Completion of the mansion was expedited in time for President James Monroe's visit to inspect the *SS Savannah* just prior to its 10,000 mile journey across the Atlantic Ocean.

Enter the property through the rear garden, the largest enclosed garden in the Historic District. Museum visits begin and end in the Gift Shop, where admission is purchased and shopping awaits the end of your tour. Parents will want to ask for the Gallery Search Sheet, a treasure hunt of sorts for youngsters visiting the museum. Teachers should call ahead to schedule special educational programs.

The collections of large, beautifully crafted models of ships are located in several galleries on two floors. Many of these ships sailed the Savannah River and many were named Savannah. The first Gallery includes a model of the *Anne*, a 200-ton British galley ship which delivered the first colonists to Georgia on February 12, 1733. Also located here is a model of the *SS Savannah*. On the main and upper floors is a special focus on the ships of the Ocean Steamship Company of Savannah. A cross section of the passenger vessel, *Kansas*, provides views of the inside, complete with crew members at work. Particularly intriguing is the upstairs gallery model of the *Titanic* as it is beginning to sink. A video reconstructing the tragic accident enhances the experience.

Exhibits upstairs also include samples of scrimshaw, a pastime said to prevent death by boredom at sea. Children will be intrigued by a Surgeon's Kit, rat trap, pins and balls for Nine Pins, and navigational instruments. One curiosity is a napkin! The napkin is actually the loose tassels on the end of a thick rope which would hang in the galley. Sailors would grab the tasseled end to wipe their hands and mouths. An elaborate valentine crafted by a sailor from shells and items found on board a ship is also on display.

The ground floor features a ship's wheel which children will enjoy turning. Restrooms are also located on this floor.

Last stop at this Museum is the Gift Shop, where adults and children will want to linger. Time and energy permitting, your next stop might be nearby River Street for an up-close view of the Savannah River channel and a possible sighting of a large, modern-day vessel.

Visitors with very young children and infants should note that this museum building is three stories with no elevator.

TELFAIR MUSEUM OF ART: TELFAIR ACADEMY OF ARTS AND SCIENCES AND JEPSON CENTER FOR THE ARTS

Academy: 121 Barnard Street on Telfair Square
Jepson Center: 207 West York Street on Telfair Square
912-790-8800
www.telfair.org
www.telfairartyfacts.org

■ ■

DAYS/HOURS OF OPERATION
Monday: Noon to 5 p.m.
Tuesday - Saturday: 10 a.m. to 5 p.m.
Sunday: 1 p.m. to 5 p.m.

ADMISSION
Telfair members free
$10 per adult, $8 per senior citizen
$4 per student K - 12
$5 per college student
$25 per family (2 adults, 2 children)
$30 per family for all three Telfair sites (2 adults, 2 children)
$15 per adult for all three Telfair sites
Children under 5 free
Discounts for AAA and military
Discounted group rates are available

Café: Monday 12 to 3 p.m., Tuesday-Saturday, 10 a.m. to 3 p.m.

FACILITIES
Café (see hours above)
Elevator
Gift Shop
Handicapped accessible
Restrooms
Special interactive website for children and teachers

47

SPECIAL EVENTS

Lectures and docent tours
Special classes
Birthday parties

"The museum is cool. I like it here because
I can make a lot of noise."

Surrena Sammons Copeland, age 4

"I have a favorite painting here, a little girl in a room with an
open door behind her. My grandma takes me here."

Katie Ratterree, age 4

The Telfair Museum of Art is three museums under one umbrella organization. One of these, the Owens-Thomas House, is an 1817 period house museum in a Regency-style mansion featured on page 117. The other two are the Telfair Academy and the Jepson Center for the Arts, both located on Telfair Square.

The Telfair Academy was built in 1819 as a home and remodeled as a museum in 1886. Until recently, the Academy was the primary display space for the Telfair's decorative and fine arts collections and special exhibitions. The Jepson Center for the Arts, which opened in 2006 as the newest addition to the Telfair complex, adds gallery space, a café, classrooms and a gift shop in a state-of-the-art building designed by Moshe Safdie.

Neighboring locations on Telfair Square provide an opportunity to span three centuries of art in one visit. As much as the Academy building reflects the classicism of the 19th century, the Jepson Center articulates the twenty-first. Even the Telfair buildings are works of art.

Visitors approaching the Jepson may be surprised to realize that the facade is glass rather than open. An impressive flight of stairs beckons from the atrium, leading upstairs to ArtZeum, an interactive two-storied space designed specifically for children of all ages. Adults be warned: ArtZeum is as much fun for grown-ups as it is for kids.

In this vibrant space which appears to be in the treetops, there are 16 displays that present art in its many forms, and just as many opportunities to create your own masterpiece. Children will be having too much fun to know that they are learning what art is, how we value it, how we look at art and why people create art. Visitors can hear from artists, wear an architectural hat or a Chinese robe or Indian tunic, create a streetscape, sit on artsy furniture and look at art books, build a city block of blocks, or walk through a glass house that is itself a work of art. A magnetic wall awaits the clanging construction of pots, pans, hardware and other metal objects into unique creations. Noise in the ArtZeum is welcome - squeals of delight are evidence that art is fun.

The Technology and Art gallery keeps viewers current on the creative techniques of time lapse technology. Plan to linger here as children are fascinated by the effects on the screen of their own motion, captured by tiny cameras. Telfair also hosts a special interactive website, www.telfairartyfacts.org, for children and teachers.

The Academy building houses the Museum's permanent collection of fine and decorative arts in galleries and period rooms. Designed by English Regency architect William Jay, it reflects one of Savannah's finest periods of architecture. Visitors are greeted by a welcoming committee of larger-than-life statues of Phidias, Rubens, Raphael, Michelangelo and Rembrandt. Inside, a stately grandeur recalls the nineteenth century and provides an impressive backdrop for paintings, sculpture and decorative arts of this earlier period. Children will enjoy imagining what it must have been like to enter when this was a home.

Ask for gallery guides for children, and allow an hour and a half to two hours for both buildings. School and special groups will benefit from an extensive array of age-appropriate activities. Your visit may coincide with one of the special programs or events, so be sure and check the website. You can eat at Telfair Cafe or venture out into the neighborhood, where there are several dining options.

MRS. WILKES' BOARDING HOUSE

107 West Jones Street
Savannah, GA 31401
(912) 232-5997
www.mrswilkes.com

- -

DAYS/HOURS OF OPERATION
Monday - Friday: Lunch, 11 a.m. - 2 p.m.
Closed in January

COST
$13 Lunch

FACILITIES
Restaurant
Restrooms

HINTS
* Allow 15 to 45 minutes for waiting in line
* Bring an umbrella in case it rains, as the wait is outside
* Go early with small children
* Groups of 30 or more can be accommodated at night with
  advance reservations

"This is my favorite place to eat in town."
Mary Ellen McKee, age 12

Standing in line may be a test of patience, but the meal here is always worth the wait. Children will enjoy the family-style seating, ten to twelve at a table in true boarding house fashion. With up to seventeen different dishes at lunchtime, even the pickiest eaters will find something to enjoy. Homestyle, Southern cooking is Mrs. Wilkes' specialty with platters and bowls heaped high with mashed potatoes, fried chicken, fish, rice, gravy, dressing, all sorts of vegetables, biscuits, dessert, and more.

Mrs. Wilkes' Dining Room is located on the ground floor of a historic paired residence on West Jones Street. Built in 1870, the house was bought and restored by Mr. and Mrs. Wilkes in 1965, the first home to be restored in an area that was fast becoming a slum. Built of Savannah grey brick, the house features double curving steps and cast iron trim.

How did Mrs. Wilkes come to operate such a successful dining room? Her story begins during World War II when the U.S. government bought her farm in Vidalia for an airstrip. She moved to Savannah and took a room in Mrs. Dixon's Boarding House on Jones Street. Shortly afterwards, she began helping Mrs. Dixon with the cooking for her boarders. Eventually, Mrs. Wilkes ran the Dining Room and the Boarding House, which led to ownership.

For many years Mrs. Wilkes fed only her boarders, but the demand for her cooking led her to open to a limited public. Today, Mrs. Wilkes serves up to 250 people a day and enjoys an international reputation as a famous Southern cook. She has been featured in magazines such as *Esquire, TIME, Brown's Guide To Georgia,* and *Redbook.*

Mrs. Wilkes' award-winning dining room has been family operated since the 1940s with the stated secret, "Never serve food that has not been sampled before leaving the kitchen."

EAST SAVANNAH, ISLANDS, AND TYBEE

∎∎

1. Fort Pulaski National Monument
2. McQueen's Island Trail/Tybee Rails to Trails
3. Oatland Island Education Center
4. Old Fort Jackson
5. Tybee Island Marine Science Center
6. Tybee Lighthouse/ Tybee Museum
7. Walter Parker Pier and Pavilion (Tybee)

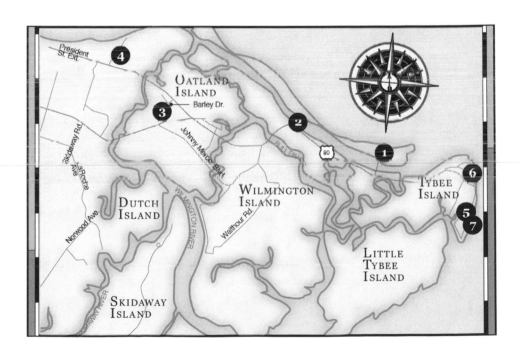

FORT PULASKI
NATIONAL MONUMENT

U.S. Department of the Interior, National Park Service
P.O. Box 30757
Location: Cockspur Island, Highway 80 East
Savannah, GA 31410-0757
(912) 786-5787
www.nps.gov/fopu

■■■

DAYS/HOURS OF OPERATION
Open daily except December 25: 9 a.m. - 5 p.m.
Hours may be extended during Summer; call for details

ADMISSION
$3 per person ages 16 and over
Children 15 and under, free

FACILITIES
Boat launching ramp
Bookstore
Fishing
Handicapped access; wheelchair available for use; audiotape for
    blind; transcripts for hearing impaired
Parking
Picnic area
Restrooms
Trails
Visitor Center
Water fountains

SPECIAL EVENTS
April: Siege and Reduction Weekend, usually between April 1 and 10
July 4th: Meridian Musket Salute
August 25th (National Parks Day): Special Programs
Labor Day Weekend: Encampment

Weekend before Christmas, Confederate Nog Party of 1861,
Candlelight Tour of Fort. Reservations required.

HINTS
* Picnic (allowed only in picnic area)
* Bug Spray
* Comfortable shoes
* Allow 1 to 2 hours for fort tour; 3 to 4 hours for fort plus picnic
and trail
* The fort was built for war, not safety. Watch your step and stay
off mounds and topmost walls
* Birthday parties and special groups welcome; advance notice
requested

"I liked best the draw-bridge, the cannons upstairs and
downstairs, and the water fountain. The fort is neat.
The fort men, the benches, and oh yeah, the moat. And
the draw-bridge you can go across, it can wind up."

Billy McKee, age 4

This castle-like fort, completed in 1847, will capture the imagination of
children of all ages. The fort took 18 years to build. In the early part of his
career, Robert E. Lee, working for the Corps of Engineers, was second in
command in overseeing the construction of the fort. It was Lee who desig-

nated the specific site for Fort Pulaski and who developed the dike and drainage system for the fort. General Lee returned to Fort Pulaski during the Civil War to command the Confederate defense of the fort.

Considered at the time of construction to be a state-of-the-art facility, Fort Pulaski's vulnerability to the all-new rifled cannon marked the end of an era in fort construction. The pentagon-shaped fort still retains its original character, and the visitor will want to allow plenty of time to explore.

Located on Cockspur Island, about 15 miles east of Savannah, Fort Pulaski became a national monument in 1924. It is named for Count Casimir Pulaski, a Polish hero who fought in the American Revolution and who was mortally wounded in the 1779 Battle of Savannah. The opportunities for a day's adventure include a nature walk, picnic, a visit to the bookstore, history lessons, and imaginative adventure.

The fort's impressive masonry structure is built of 25 million bricks. The moat surrounding the fort holds the promise of a few wild alligators, and two draw-bridges give Fort Pulaski fairy-tale security. Take time to explore the maze of underground tunnels, rooms and niches after crossing the first draw-bridge. Just past the second draw-bridge, examine the massive doors made of Georgia heart pine.

Once inside the fort, there are two levels around a large open area with a grassy parade ground in the center. Cannons, a prison, soldiers' quarters with beds and mattresses stuffed with straw all portray the life of the soldier. From the upper level of the fort, visitors can view the mouth of the Savannah River as it enters the Atlantic Ocean. On a clear day, Daufuskie, Hilton Head, and Tybee Islands are also visible. Visitors should watch children on the upper level of the fort, for there are no rails or safety guards to prevent a fall.

Benches on the parade grounds are shaded by two large pecan trees. Interpretive programs are given here at announced times. Close by are restrooms, water fountains, and a cannon. This is a wonderful place for children to play after touring the fort.

The visitor's center is a combination bookstore, museum, and information center. Maps, daily information on programs, and a 15-minute video help to orient the visitor. The shop has an unusual array of Confederate flags and a number of books about the Confederacy, forts, and history.

A hiking trail (.6 mile) leads from the parking lot to the picnic area. The trail is easy to follow with interpretive signs along the way and travels through woods and open, grassy areas where deer might be visible. Snakes and alligators are possibilities, and it is best to stay on the trail. Three detours at the outset of the trail include the old North Pier, Battery Hambright, and Wesley Memorial. The picnic area, shaded by pine and palmetto trees, is clean and well-kept with more than a dozen picnic tables. Parking, restrooms, trash cans, and the occasional river breeze make this area a perfect picnic spot.

MCQUEENS ISLAND TRAIL/ TYBEE RAILS TO TRAILS

Managed by Chatham County Public Works and Park Services Dept.
P.O. Box 8161
Savannah, GA 31412
Location address: U.S. Highway 80 East
(912) 652-6786, 652-6780
www.chathamcounty.org/pwrs_recreationmain.html

■■■

DAYS/HOURS OF OPERATION
Daily: sunup to sundown

ADMISSION
Free

FACILITIES
Exercise stations
Handicapped access
Parking
Picnic facilities
Portable Toilets

HINTS
* Bring bug spray
* Wear comfortable shoes
* Plan a picnic
* Be alert for snakes

"It's neat, but hot (in the summer)!"
Billy McKee, age 5

A testimony to the success of volunteers and the commitment of the Chatham County Public Works and Park Services Department, this six-and-a-half mile long trail is a delightful way to exercise while enjoying the abundant wildlife and scenic views. Following an abandoned railway, this multi-purpose trail is designed for cycling, jogging, walking and camping. There are nine fitness stations along the scenic and historic trail.

Located on the railway line which once connected Savannah to Tybee Island, this line was abandoned in the 1930s due to the popularity of car travel. The trail itself is part of a national system of trails known as the Conversion of Rails to Trails, and this organization designated the McQueens Island Trail one of America's first 500 Rail Trails.

The trail runs west to east from Elba Creek to the Lazaretto Creek Boat Ramp Park. Children should be accompanied by adults along the entire length of the trail because there are rattlesnakes present in the area. A 175-foot long fishing pier with parking in the South Channel holds the promise of flounder or trout for supper.

Picnics should be packed for easy carrying, as the trail is long. Hats and sunscreen are "musts" on this sunny corridor.

OATLAND ISLAND
WILDLIFE CENTER OF SAVANNAH

Owned and managed by the Savannah/Chatham County Public Schools
711 Sandtown Road
Savannah, GA 31410
(912) 898-3980
www.oatlandisland.org

DAYS/HOURS OF OPERATION
Everyday: 9 a.m. to 4 p.m.
Closed Thanksgiving, Christmas and New Year's Day

ADMISSION
$5 for ages 17 and older
$3 for children ages 4-17, Senior Citizens and Military
Children 3 and under are free

FACILITIES
Drinks Available
Gift Shop
Parking
Picnic area
Restrooms
Trails

SPECIAL EVENTS
September: Medieval Festival
October: Halloween Hike
November: Cane Grinding Festival
March: Sheep to Shawl

HINTS
* Allow at least 3 hours to include a picnic
* May be tiring for younger children; bring stroller or baby carrier
* Bring bug spray
* Bring extra drinks, snacks
* Gates are locked at 5 p.m.

"I liked seeing especially the bald eagle and the huge alligator."

Billy McKee, age 5

Oatland Island Wildlife Center is a unique and special experience for children of all ages. Operating as an environmental education center, Oatland is maintained by the Savannah/Chatham County Public School System. It is not a zoo, but it does provide the opportunity to see native animals and birds of coastal Georgia in their natural habitat. Some of these animals are threatened or endangered; some have been injured and cannot be returned to the wild.

Oatland Island, with its 175-acres, is committed to wildlife conservation and educating children about coastal Georgia's native animals. The Center has been awarded national and international certification as a supplementary school.

Following the nature trail will give the visitor a full view of Oatland Island's delightful animal experiences. Trail guides are available in the Main Building. Trails are well marked and well traveled, with educational markers at the various animal habitats.

Highlights of the trail include close-up views of a pair of endangered bald eagles, and the opportunity to view the rare Florida panther. Other animals at Oatland which are rarely seen in the wild by humans include gray wolves, black bear, red fox, bobcats, and other small mammals. A pair of bison are some of Oatland's largest residents which nowadays can be seen only in national parks or on private lands. Four different types of owls - the screech owl, the barred owl, the horned owl and the barn owl - will engage the visitor in a staring contest. Alligators are viewed in their natural habitat, and an elevated boardwalk leads visitors out of the woods and into the salt marsh.

The barnyard area portrays animal life on a farm with a pig, cow, chickens, goats, rabbits, sheep, and turkeys. Tucked away in a clearing in the forest is the Heritage Homesite area where two restored 1835 log cabins provide a rustic spot for educational programs and the annual fall Cane Grinding and spring Sheep Shearing Festivals.

Oatland Island is open for public and private schools as well as for the general public. Guided tours and special programs are available with advance reservations. The animals and birds in their natural habitats have much to teach visitors of all ages in Oatland's unique learning environment.

OLD FORT JACKSON

Managed by Coastal Heritage Society
1 Fort Jackson Road
Savannah, GA 31404
(912) 232-3945
www.chsgeorgia.org

DAYS/HOURS OF OPERATION
7 days per week: 9 a.m. - 5 p.m.
Closed Thanksgiving, Christmas, New Year's Day

ADMISSION
$4.25 per adult
$3.75 per child, 6 to 11, senior citizens

FACILITIES
Drink machines
Gift shop
Handicapped access
Leashed pets allowed
Parking
Picnic area
Restrooms
Shelter
Visitors Center

HINTS
* Bug Spray
* Take a picnic
* Allow one and one half hours
* Great place for parties. A cannon-firing is a hallmark of planned
  parties.

*"This is one of my favorite places to visit because you
can run around and play pretend war."*

Joe Ratterree, age 8

"My brother had his birthday party here once, and we dressed up like soldiers. Sometimes a huge ship comes by the fort."

Katie Ratterree, age 4

Old Fort Jackson is located three miles from Savannah at a point on the Savannah River where all channels converge. Every ship entering or leaving the port of Savannah passes here. Today, this almost surely guarantees a glimpse of a huge container ship. A century and a half earlier, however, this strategic location had great potential for coastal defense. This is exactly what President Jefferson had in mind in 1808 when construction of the fort was begun on what was formerly a colonial brickyard and Revolutionary War earthworks. The Fort as it is seen today was built in two major phases, the second being completed in time for the Civil War.

The Orientation Center near the parking lot is the old depot building for the Tybee Railroad. Formerly located closer to Savannah, the structure was moved to the Fort in 1989. Here visitors purchase their admission tickets. The gift shop is worth a stop on the way out. Visitors walk along a Belgian block pathway to the river where markers explain the historic events that occurred on or near the site. The large open area to the right is the site of former rice fields.

Another path leads to the fort where visitors enter in nineteenth-century fashion via a draw-bridge. Cannon-firing demonstrations take place in the center area which is flanked on both sides by barracks foundations and covered pavilions. A stairway leads up to a parapet where a large cannon is located. The sweeping view from here illustrates why this site was so attractive for river defense.

Beneath the parapet an enclosed exhibit area features many displays that interpret the fort's history. Children enjoy wandering through the tunnels and alcoves inside. The first stop should be the small room with an audio-visual presentation which is self-activated. This 20-minute overview is most informative. Military uniforms, weapons from various eras, and collections of artifacts are displayed in the alcoves which provide structural support for the weight of the parapet overhead. Of particular interest are two models of Fort Jackson, one circa 1812 and the other, 1864. These clarify the phases of the construction that took place between 1808 and 1864.

TYBEE ISLAND MARINE SCIENCE CENTER

1510 Strand
P.O. Box 1879
Tybee Island, GA 31328
(912) 786-5917
www.tybeemsc.org
Located in the beach parking lot accessed on 14th Street,
  near the public pier and pavilion

- -

DAYS/HOURS OF OPERATION
Open daily 9 a.m. - 5 p.m.,
  except closed at Noon on Tuesdays

ADMISSION
$4 per adult
$3 per child ages 3 to 16 years
Free for children 2 years or younger
Free for members
Discounts for seniors, military families,
  and students with identification

FACILITIES
Gift Shop
Restrooms

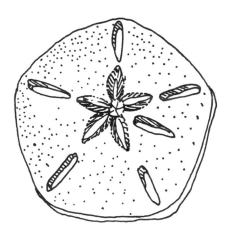

SPECIAL EVENTS
Beach & Marsh Discovery Walks
Boo at the Beach
Children's Video Series
Field trips for all ages
Scout Patch Programs
Summer Sea Camp
Turtle Trot & Celebration
Tuesday Guest Lecture Series
Tybee Turtle Talks
Whale of a Weekend

"My favorite thing about this visit was seeing the sharks' teeth."

Ben Beason, age 14

The Tybee Island Marine Science Center features marine life from coastal Georgia. The aquariums and exhibits are home to a variety of fish, reptiles, invertebrates, corals, and other interesting sea creatures. The touch-tank encourages hands to pick up and examine live whelks, hermit crabs, and horseshoe crabs. The dry sand table allows visitors to identify shells commonly found on the Tybee shore.

Rows of teeth in the wide open jaws of several shark species impress even the youngest visitor. Northern right whales migrate past Georgia's coast each year. Whale artifacts are on display, as well as information on the bottlenose dolphin, a year round resident. After learning about the loggerhead sea turtles that nest on Tybee's beach, visitors can name a future hatchling through the Adopt-an-Egg program. A large Gray's Reef aquarium, sponsored by the National Marine Sanctuary, shows the many varieties of marine life that inhabit the reef.

Exploring the exhibits is just one of many things to do at the Science Center. Before planning a trip, call ahead or visit the website for information on scheduled beach and marsh walks, summer sea camp, special guest lectures and events, such as the Whale of a Weekend or the Turtle Trot and Celebration.

The Marine Science Center is located in the beach parking lot between 14th and Tybrisa (16th) Street. The front door faces the ocean, inviting beachcombers to bring in their "finds" for identification.

TYBEE LIGHTHOUSE/TYBEE MUSEUM

Tybee Island Historical Society
30 Meddin Drive
P.O. Box 366
Tybee Island, GA 31328
(912) 786-5801
www.tybeelighthouse.org

■ ■

DAYS/HOURS OF OPERATION
9 a.m. - 5:30 p.m. daily, last ticket sold at 4:30 p.m.
Closed Tuesdays and major holidays

ADMISSION
$6 per adult
$5 per child, 6-12
Children under 6, free
$5 per senior citizen

FACILITIES
Drink machine
Museum Store
Parking
Restrooms

HINTS
* Sunscreen
* Cool drinks, during summer
* Allow two hours

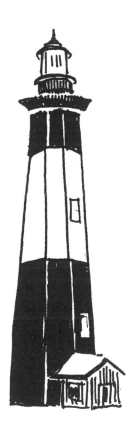

"My favorite thing about this visit was the little pirate guns at the museum and the model of the circle! I liked going to the top of the lighthouse and looking at the ocean and going up the stairs and counting them."

Billy McKee, age 4

Going to the beach is usually appealing to children of all ages. With the additional attraction of a lighthouse and a museum in an old fort, enthusiasm doubles. Located on the northern tip of Tybee Island, the lighthouse was first established in 1736, just three years after James Oglethorpe settled on the Savannah River. Although the lighthouse standing today is not the original, the lower sixty feet were constructed in 1773, and the upper ninety-four feet date to 1867. A beacon, the original Fresnal lens from 1867, shines at the top of the lighthouse, which can be seen eighteen miles away.

Children and energetic adults will enjoy the 178-step climb to the top of the tower. The view from the top of the lighthouse on a clear day stretches for miles in all directions, although it takes a stout-hearted person to stand for long on the narrow metal ledge which encircles the top.

Lighthouses carry an aura of historical romance about them. The Tybee light is no exception. It has seen two major wars - the Revolutionary War and the Civil War - and countless storms and hurricanes. Yet, the Tybee light continues to shine, greeting Savannah port visitors as they enter the mouth of the Savannah River. The lighthouse anchors a five-acre site with six historical buildings which include the lighthouse keeper's cottage, separate kitchen, an oil house, the first assistant keeper's cottage, and soldier's barracks from the Civil War.

The lighthouse is owned and maintained by the Tybee Island Historical Society.

Across the street from the lighthouse is the **TYBEE MUSEUM**. Located in part of Old Fort Screven, built in 1899, the museum's drab stucco exterior was designed to merge with the sandy beach landscape. At one time the batteries were covered to look like a sand dune in the effort to camouflage the fort.

Battery Garland houses the museum, and the network of small rooms and narrow stairways, halls and small angular windows will fulfill a child's desire to explore and discover. Numerous exhibits fill the museum. One details the history of Fort Screven, another the construction of the Martello Tower on Tybee which began in 1815. Panoramas, dioramas, paintings, Native American displays, historic diving equipment, and historical artifacts fill the maze of rooms. Visitors will end at a narrow stairway which leads to the roof. Although railings are present, it is best to keep young children by the hand and in close view. The observation deck on the roof provides a great view of the Savannah River entrance and the Atlantic Ocean.

Parking is plentiful with a boardwalk to the beach from the museum. Like the lighthouse, the museum is operated by the Tybee Island Historical Society, a non-profit organization.

WALTER PARKER PIER AND PAVILION

End of 16th Street
Tybee Island, Georgia 31328
(912) 786-6780
www.chathamcounty.org/pwps_pavilion.html

■ ■

DAYS/HOURS OF OPERATION
Pier: 6 a.m. to 11 p.m. daily
Pavilion: 10 a.m. to 11 p.m. daily

ADMISSION
Free

FACILITIES
Boardwalk
Covered picnic area
Drink Machines
Handicapped Accessible
Restrooms
Snack Bar

SPECIAL EVENTS
Groups may reserve pavilion. Special rates are available for non-profits.

HINTS
* No pets, bikes, or skates allowed
* Perfect for a break from the sun and an ice cream or sno-cone treat

"It's fun to be here at night. It's neat being out really
far over the ocean."

Darr Smith, age 8

"The ice cream's really good and it's fun watching
the fishers fish."

Hunter Smith, age 7

The Walter Parker Pier and Pavilion at Tybee Island offers respite from a hot summer sun or unexpected rain showers. Picnic tables, cold drinks, ice cream, and the best view of the ocean entice families with children.

Fishermen lounge in chairs and on the rails along the pier waiting for a nibble. While strolling the pier, someone may get an interesting catch - catfish, stingray, flounder, shark, or toadfish. Children will enjoy talking with the fishermen, who are generally relaxed and like to share a "fish" story. Some of the fishermen even carry along pictures of their previous catches!

The pier and pavilion were built in 1996, standing where the old Tybrisa Pavilion stood. The original was built in the 1891 by the Central of Georgia Railroad and destroyed by fire in 1967.

Fishing requires a permit, but may be a fun activity, particularly in the late summer and early fall when the shrimp are plentiful.

Nearby is the Tybee Island Marine Science Center which is another pleasant diversion from sand and sun.

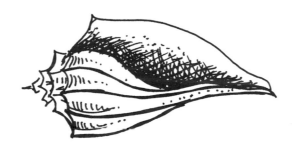

MIDTOWN AND SOUTHWEST SAVANNAH

1. The Bamboo Farm
2. Daffin Park
3. Hull Park
4. L. Scott Stell Park
5. Mighty Eighth Air Force Museum
6. Savannah Ogeechee Canal Museum & Nature Center
7. Tom Triplett Community Park

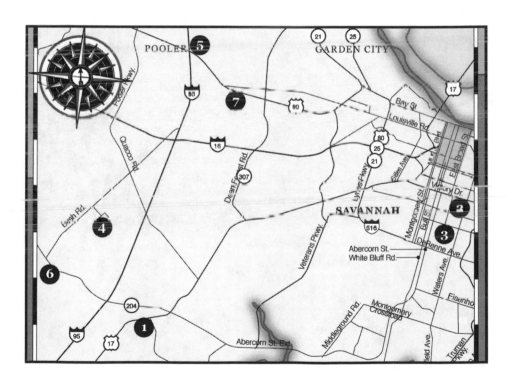

THE BAMBOO FARM AND COASTAL GARDENS

Operated by University of Georgia Cooperative Extension Service
  with Chatham County
2 Canebrake Road
Savannah, GA 31419
(912) 921-5460
www.bamboo.caes.uga.edu

DAYS/HOURS OF OPERATION
Monday through Friday: 8 a.m. to 5 p.m.
Saturday: 10 a.m. to 5 p.m.
Sunday: Noon to 5

ADMISSION
Free; donations welcome

FACILITIES
Catering Kitchen
Conference Center and Classrooms
Parking (free)
Picnic areas, including a pavilion that seats 600
Restrooms
Trails
Vending machines

HINTS
* Plan a picnic
* Good place for birthday parties
* Bug spray and sun screen
* Outdoor shoes
* Allow one hour minimum

"I heard lots of bees buzzing and I watched out for them. They were on the flowers. I liked walking on the wood (flower bed borders)."

Katie Ratterree, age 3

Curiosity about the name may prompt a visit to the Bamboo Farm, which features the largest collection of bamboo open for public viewing in the United States. It was established in 1919 by the U.S. Department of Agriculture for the introduction of oriental and other non-native seeds and plants. New species of plants were studied for their adaptability to the coastal climate, and bamboo is one of many plants that thrived. For several years, the bamboo grown here was shipped to zoos around the United States and Canada to feed panda bears.

Today the site is the Coastal Area Extension Center for the University of Georgia Cooperative Extension Service. It is open to the public year round and features many plants that thrive in this agricultural zone. In addition to the bamboo collection, the 46-acre site includes a cottage garden, a xeriscape garden, a butterfly garden, strawberry fields, two lakes (one features a large covered pavilion), greenhouses, a compost exhibit and a conference center. Food crops are developed on a seasonal basis, and trees and shrubs are grown also. The Bamboo Farm is a good place for children to learn about ecology in a pleasant outdoor setting.

During spring and summer, beds of annuals, perennials and herbs offer dazzling displays of color and pleasant aromas. Roses, daylilies, dianthus, zinnias, herbs, petunias, and sunflowers not only appeal to the viewer but also attract bees, so care should be taken with young children. There is a handout which guides visitors and also describes specimen trees and shrubs.

There is a lakeside picnic area with a 30' x 30' deck over the water. Bamboo has been put to use everywhere: as a decorative treatment for trash containers and planter boxes, as well as for fencing, path borders and trellises. Parking is free and there are spaces designated for handicapped parking. Paths throughout the various areas are not paved, but there are no obstacles for wheelchairs.

The small office near the parking lot is a good place to begin a visit. Staff and volunteers are available for organized group tours. The Roots and Shoots program is designed for K through 5th grade and is an excellent school outing. Blackberry and strawberry picking are seasonal activities that will entertain children and may produce enough fruit to nibble now and bake into a pie later. Fishing is allowed May through September, and there are several annual events that are children- and family-focused. Any time of year, a visit to the Bamboo Farm will be more enjoyable for young (ages 3 to 8) children if there is a plan: a picnic, crayons and paper for drawing and coloring, a species hunt or a color search.

Time permitting, visitors to the Bamboo Farm may want to continue south on Highway 17 to Fort McAllister, Fort Morris or Midway, for a full day of coastal adventure.

DAFFIN PARK

1301 East Victory Drive
Savannah, GA 31405
(912) 351-3837, (912) 351-3841
www.savannahga.gov

DAYS/HOURS OF OPERATION
Sunup - 9 p.m.

ADMISSION
Free for park; hourly fees for tennis courts; rental fee for pavilion
use or exclusive use of any park area

FACILITIES
Baseball diamonds
Basketball court
Fishing
Football fields
Handicapped access
Parking
Pets on leash
Picnic area
Playground
Pond
Restrooms (accessible for handicapped)
Shelter
Swimming pool
Soccer fields
Stadium
Tennis courts
Track (1.5 miles)

HINTS
* Events take place here year-round
* Great place for birthday parties
* Bug spray during spring and fall
* Baseball season provides opportunities for stadium parties;
  call 351-9150 for more information on special baseball parties

"You can see fish swimming in the pond. In the pavilion you feel like you are on an island."

Katie Ratterree, age 4

In a city which clearly loves parks, Daffin Park is one of the most diverse. Few parks in the city can claim Daffin's combination of natural beauty and wide variety of recreational amenities. Its central location along the palm-and live oak-planted Victory Drive makes this park accessible to many neighborhoods.

The 77-acre park was begun in 1907. The original plan, drawn by landscape architect John Nolen, has adapted well over the years to the community's growing recreational needs. The park is named for P. D. Daffin, who was Chairman of the Park and Tree Commission for 31 years, until his death in 1929.

Avenues of live oak trees define the park space and provide shade to drives and walkways. The center of the park is encircled by a drive and flanked by tennis courts, a swimming pool, and playing fields used for rugby, soccer, baseball, softball, and football. The western end of Daffin features an attractive, fenced playground that is accessible for the physically handicapped and wheelchairs. Along Victory Drive, there is a large pond with a covered pavilion in its center. The most prominent features of the pond are its two fountains, which shoot enormous sprays of water into the air. In recent years, the Rotary Club of Savannah has adopted the pond as a project and has been responsible for enhancing its beauty with the fountains, sidewalks, and lighting. The pond is also stocked with fish.

The eastern section of the park consists mainly of Grayson Stadium. This structure was built in the 1940s on the site of an earlier, wooden stadium that was destroyed in a major hurricane in August, 1940. Today, Grayson Stadium is home to the Savannah Sand Gnats, a South Atlantic minor league team. Near the stadium are picnic areas within a grove of pine trees named the Herty Forest for Dr. Charles Herty. A jogging path of 1.5 miles encircles the entire park.

Mornings at Daffin find walkers, joggers, and pre-schoolers. Afternoons, the playing fields come to life with team sports. The tennis courts are popular year-round, all day long. Youth-league sports and home baseball games bring the park to life at night. For all ages, Daffin Park is one of Savannah's most popular destinations.

HULL PARK

912-651-6786
Atlantic Avenue at 55th Street
Savannah, GA 31405
www.savannahga.gov

■■

DAYS/HOURS OF OPERATION
Daylight to 9 p.m.

ADMISSION
Free for general park use
Fee for parties

FACILITIES
Amphitheatre
Free parking
Handicapped accessible
Pavilion with picnic tables
Pets allowed on leash
Playground
Shelter
Sprinkler spray pool (seasonal)
Trash receptacles
Water fountain

HINTS
* Birthday parties allowed, reservations required
    ($30 fee to reserve pavilion)
* No alcohol or glass containers are allowed
* Summer lunch program provided here with free meals
    for children under 18
* Supervised hours
* Arts and crafts activities in summer

"I like playing on the slide and going on the baby swings. And running in the sprinklers. And I love to go up the ladders."

Mary Jo Lavanish, age 3

City-owned Hull Park is a medium-sized, diamond-shaped space nestled inside an Ardsley Park neighborhood, off the beaten track of heavily traveled streets. Frequented primarily by those who live in the general area, it is also a favorite destination for others seeking a safe open area with lots of options for children.

Hull Park features a well-equipped playground, covered pavilion area with picnic tables, sidewalks for bicycling and skating, grassy areas for pick-up games and a baseball diamond. The swings accommodate various ages and sizes of children.

This park also has an amphitheatre and spray pool, which is operated to the delight of youngsters during the summer months. (There is a $10 per hour fee for the spray pool at other times). Mothers can sit on the steps of the amphitheatre and keep a watchful eye on both the spray pool and the playground. This is a good park for groups of children, and a favorite stop for school field trips.

During the summer months, the City of Savannah serves free lunches at Hull Park to children under the age of 18. Hull Park playground is staffed during afternoons and for extended hours during the summer. There is not abundant shade here, so the picnic tables beneath the covered pavilion are popular.

A visit to Hull Park can be a stand-alone outing, or a place to come for a picnic after a visit elsewhere, such as a museum or the Aquatic Center. Mornings are cooler. No restrooms exist here, so plan ahead.

L. SCOTT STELL COMMUNITY PARK

383 Bush Road
Savannah, GA 31419
(912) 925-8694 / 921-0039
www.chathamcounty.org/pwrs recreationmain.html

DAYS/HOURS OF OPERATION
Spring and Summer: 8 a.m. - 11 p.m.
Fall and Winter: 8 a.m. - 10 p.m.

ADMISSION
Free

FACILITIES
Bike trail
Camping (through special arrangements)
Handicapped access
Office
Parking
Picnic areas
Restrooms
Shelters
Snack Bar during sports games
Sports field and courts

SPECIAL EVENTS
Halloween Haunted House
Plant Your Own Garden
Family Flea Market
Fishing Rodeo
Easter Egg Hunt

HINTS
* Bring a picnic or snack
* Bring dirt bikes
* Bring some bait for fishing
* Might want lawn chairs

"We liked seeing the ducks on the lake and we wanted our bikes for the bike trail."

Tom McKee, age 10
Tony Zabarac, age 10

Chatham County's L. Scott Stell Community Park, tucked away between Highway 204 and Littleneck Road, is a gem of a park. Spread out over 108 acres, this park formerly served the federal government as a helicopter training field during the Vietnam War. The roads in the park are the old runways, and park officials continue to refer to them as runways. Landing markers and painted lines from practice days are still visible. Even the tennis courts are built on a section of the old runway. Called the Ogeechee State Field, this land was transferred to Chatham County from the federal government for $1.00.

Children will enjoy feeding or watching the ducks which swim on the man-made S-shaped lake. Surrounding the lake is a one-mile jogging/hiking trail for exercising or a casual stroll. Fishing is free, and the lake is stocked with bass, crappie, catfish, and bream.

There is a playground near two large picnic areas with a few covered pavilions.

Possibly one of the most unique features of this park is the opportunity to plant one's own garden in the 93 free garden spots located around the perimeter of one of the "runways." Park personnel see that the soil is plowed and prepared for planting. All they ask of gardeners is to plant, maintain, and harvest their crops. This is a great opportunity for children to have first-hand experience with growing their own vegetables.

Practicing baseball, soccer, tennis, and volleyball are on-going, and traffic in the park may vary according to scheduled games. There seems to be ample parking for all with lots of wide open spaces for running around, flying a kite, playing ball, and just plain having fun!

MIGHTY EIGHTH AIR FORCE MUSEUM

175 Bourne Avenue
Pooler, GA 31407
912-748-8888
www.mightyeighth.org

Located just off I-95, Exit 102, Pooler

■ ■

DAYS/HOURS OF OPERATION
Daily: 9 a.m. to 5 p.m.
Closed New Year's Day, Easter Sunday,
    Thanksgiving Day and Christmas Day

ADMISSION
$10 per adult
$9 Seniors, Military and Student
$6 ages 6 to 12
Free for children under 5

FACILITIES
Chapel
Full restaurant, Cafeteria
Gardens
Gift Shop
Handicapped access
Restrooms

HINTS
* Allow at least 30 minutes for Gift Shop with a budget
* Curriculum guides available for teachers

"I liked when we saw the huge airplane near the back near the sanctuary and also I liked the shop!"

Darr Smith, Jr., age 7

"I liked the store and I liked the guy with the gas mask. I liked the jet planes and the planes hanging up!"

Hunter Smith, age 5

Although World War II history may not sound like entertainment for young children, this museum is interactive and captivating. Huge airplanes, bombers, jets and videos will capture the imagination of all ages as well as provide a sobering history lesson.

As you walk into the museum, look up. Above your head in the rotunda is a real parachute draped from the ceiling. While you are paying admission and getting oriented, the children will be able to stand beneath this parachute and let their imaginations whirr!

The Mighty Eighth Museum honors those who served in the Eighth Air Force. Savannah is a fitting place to house the museum, as the Eighth Air Force division was activated in Savannah in 1942 at the National Guard Armory building in downtown Savannah. There is a spirit of courage and sacrifice in this museum that wraps around the visitor's experience. Each exhibit tells a story about real people - our grandfathers and grandmothers - who lived through a significant war. The Memorial Garden outside brings a reverence to most children, honoring those who fought and died in World War II.

The Walls of Valor, the Reflecting Pool, monuments erected by Eighth Air Force veterans and families, and the Chapel of the Fallen Eagles create a variety of opportunities to understand the importance of the Eighth Air Force in the European theatre of World War II. The names of people who served in the Eighth are shown on the Wall of Valor. Visitors who have family members who served will want to look for the names. Children will enjoy exploring outside and inside the Museum.

The tour ends in a wonderful Gift Shop. You will not be able to avoid this diversion, so you might as well prepare a spending budget before you get there and relax as your children decide how to spend your money! Real dog tags are inexpensive and made on the spot. They are always a hit.

Teachers will want to ask about curriculum guides and activities targeted to specific ages.

SAVANNAH OGEECHEE CANAL MUSEUM AND NATURE CENTER

681 Fort Argyle Road (Ga. Highway 204)
Savannah, GA 31419-9239
912-748-8068
www.savannahogeecheecanal.com

● ●

DAYS/HOURS OF OPERATION
7 days per week: 9 a.m. to 5 p.m.

ADMISSION
$2 per person
$1 Children ages 4 to 12
Free for members and for children ages 3 and under
Group programs are available with reservations

FACILITIES
Drink machine
Free parking off street
Handicapped accessible
Museum
Restrooms
Water fountain

HINTS
* Allow two hours for a visit
* Bug spray and sunscreen in summer months

"There are so many trails, it's hard to pick, but I like the
one that goes to the river."
Katie Ratterree, age 11

"It started raining when we were here and
it was still fun!"
Candice Aaron, age 11

"I like the snakes and reptiles the best."

Margaret Spence, age 10

The Savannah-Ogeechee (S&O) Canal Nature Center is a little off the beaten track but well worth an outing for all ages. This is a great place for a picnic, so be sure to allow two or three hours.

The S&O Canal was dug in the early 19th century as an industrial corridor to transport goods between the Savannah and Ogeechee Rivers. More than five hundred laborers worked for six years to dig the canal, which was five feet deep. Mule-drawn barges carried lumber, rice, cotton and naval stores along its 16 ½ mile length. Locks 5 and 6 can be seen on the canal property.

The 184-acre wooded site, located on the Ogeechee River, is now owned and managed by the S&O Canal Society. Many volunteers have worked to make the site accessible and educational for visitors. The entrance is located on Ft. Argyle Road (Ga. 204), on the left, 2.3 miles west of I-95.

Begin your visit by checking in at the nature center and museum, where you can pick up a brochure and a map before exploring the many trails. Tours are self directed. A covered picnic area and restrooms are located near the nature center.

Miles of beautiful trails meander through swampland, forests, an isolated sand ridge and along the banks of the Ogeechee River. Trails are named for natural features: Ridge, Holly, River and Popcorn Tree. The quickest route to the Ogeechee River is along the old toll road. Parents will want to accompany very young adventurers near the river. At low tide, sandy beaches are accessible on the Ogeechee. On one of the trails, a covered platform overlooks the river for birdwatching or resting.

The remains of old moonshine stills, a tree which has grown around a pot (the pot tree must be seen to be believed), burrows of armadillos and gopher tortoises and the support structures of the original locks are fascinating features of these trails. Children will enjoy the bridges and boardwalks that span the wet areas.

The S&O Canal is a fun place to learn history while enjoying nature in the lowcountry.

TOM TRIPLETT COMMUNITY PARK

Location: U.S. Highway 80 West
Managed by Chatham County Public Works and Park Services Dept.
P.O. Box 8161
Savannah, GA 31412
(912) 652-6780
www.chathamcounty.org/pwps_recreationmain.html

DAYS/HOURS OF OPERATION
Daily: 8 a.m. until dark
(Hours may change. Call above number for most current information)

ADMISSION
Free

FACILITIES
Bike Trail
Handicapped access
Parking
Picnic areas
Restrooms
Shelters

HINTS
* Bring drinks, snacks
* Great for biking
* Consider a fishing pole, bait
* Bug spray

"This park was fun. We found a caterpillar and it crawled on my hand."

Kelly Haas, age 6

"I like the water and the ducks and the grass and the playground."

Jake Haas, age 2

If you are looking for a rural park, Tom Triplett Community Park offers a peaceful visit away from the noise of the city. Officially opened in 1998, this park is over 200 acres, the largest park in the County's system.

Parking is plentiful and is near the restrooms and a covered picnic area. A fully-stocked, freshwater lake is surrounded by a 1½ mile paved path, which is the perfect place to begin your visit. Bring along bicycles for a faster tour of the park. Picnic tables are spaced intermittently around the lake for resting or snacking.

One of the main highlights of this park is the forest. A variety of mature hardwoods surround the lake and extend out into the park. A conservation program protects the forest, and visitors may explore a dirt trail which leads to Lock 3 of the Savannah/Ogeechee Canal. If you decide to veer off the paved trail to this dirt path through the forest, allow an extra hour and be sure to carry bug spray. It is a nice hike in dry weather, but it could be very muddy during a rainy season.

You and your children will feel like you have been out-of-town and in the woods after a visit to Tom Triplett Park. You may even hear or see a train rumbling down the nearby train tracks.

One of the park's newest and more innovative additions is a golf frisbee course. This has become very popular with frisbee enthusiasts! Future plans for the park include tennis and basketball courts and additional trails through the forest.

SOUTHEAST SAVANNAH
AND ISLANDS

1. The Aquarium at Skidaway Island
2. Bacon Park Forest
3. Bethesda Home for Boys
4. Chatham County Aquatic Center
5. Chatham County Garden Center and Botanical Gardens
6. Lake Mayer
7. Skidaway Island State Park
8. Wormsloe Historic Site

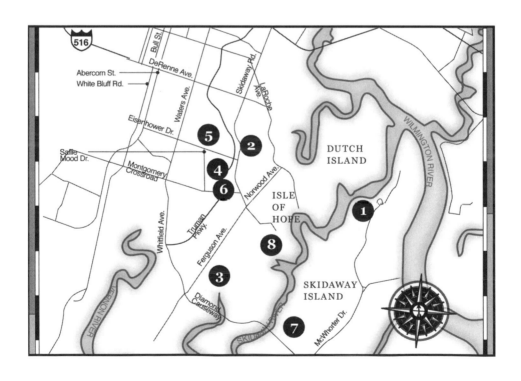

THE AQUARIUM AT SKIDAWAY ISLAND

University of Georgia Marine Extension Service
30 Ocean Science Circle
Savannah, GA 31411
(912) 598-2496
www.uga.edu/aquarium

■ ■

DAYS/HOURS OF OPERATION
Monday-Friday: 9 a.m. - 4 p.m.
Saturday: Noon - 5 p.m.

ADMISSION
$2 per person; $1 children ages 3-12 and Senior Citizens;
Children ages 1-2 are free

FACILITIES
Gift Shop
Nature Trail
Parking
Picnic area
Restrooms
Vending machines

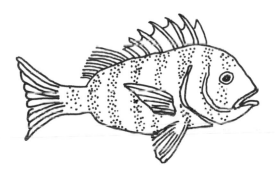

SPECIAL EVENTS
Sea Camp for children ages 4-15, with weekly sessions
  in June and July
Open House every fall (call to find out which weekend)

HINTS
* Take a picnic
* Bring bug spray
* Allow one hour for the Aquarium; add one hour for trail and picnic
* Large groups must call in advance to check on availability

"I liked looking at the sharks most. I also like the nature trail. We've seen deer on the trail before."

Joe Ratterree, age 8

The Aquarium at Skidaway Island is a favorite outing for all ages. Its beautiful setting overlooking the Skidaway River is reason enough to make this a destination, but the Aquarium offers more than scenery. The Aquarium is part of a large complex which includes The University of Georgia Marine Extension Service and the Skidaway Institute of Oceanography. While some of the facilities are reserved for research and conference purposes, the Aquarium, picnic area, and nature trail are open to the public.

Newly renovated, the Aquarium focuses on Georgia's marine and estuarine animals with regional fish of all shapes, sizes and colors. The main exhibit space, sensibly laid out and easy to follow, consists of wall tanks housing various species of fish and invertebrates. Labels are easy to read and well illustrated. Step-up platforms and handrails allow face-to-face encounters with fish, sharks, and turtles.

A favorite collection is the "herd" of seahorses, which frolic to the delight of visitors. Other exhibits at the Aquarium display historic and prehistoric uses of coastal resources, shells, skulls, and other artifacts. A favorite activity is to take crayons or markers, and draw pictures of the fish and their habitats.

It is wise to plan enough time for enjoying the Jay Wolf nature trail. Approximately one mile in length, the path takes in coastal vistas as well as woodlands. Selected native trees are clearly marked. At low tide, children enjoy walking along the marsh's edge and chasing the elusive fiddler crab, while a shaded bench overlooking the marsh and river is a tempting resting spot for grown-ups. Along the wooded part of the trail, it is not unusual to hear the footsteps of deer, and more often than not they will make a fleeting appearance.

The picnic area is located between the Aquarium and the entrance to the nature trail. Shady, cool, and offering magnificent views of the Skidaway River, this spot calls for an outing planned around meal or snack time, or even a party. Group gatherings are welcome with food limited to the picnic area.

Staff at the Aquarium are predominantly behind-the-scenes, or leading field trips for formal groups, but can be summoned from the office to answer questions or offer other assistance. A small educational sales shop offers t-shirts, local fishing maps and booklets, post cards, and collectibles.

BACON PARK FOREST

6262 Skidaway Road
Savannah, GA 31406
912-351-3837
Enter at Bacon Park Tennis Complex

DAYS/HOURS OF OPERATION
Sun-up to Sundown

ADMISSION
Free

FACILITIES
Parking
Restrooms at Tennis Center
Trails

SPECIAL EVENTS
Seasonal Discovery Walks offered by
    Savannah Tree Foundation

HINTS
* Wear old clothes and shoes
* Bring bug spray
* Allow an hour

"The wildflowers were cool."
Kelly Haas, age 6

"Look at the squirrels so high!"
Jake Haas, age 2

Bacon Park Forest is a pleasant surprise in an urban setting. This 50-acre inland maritime forest is a rare pastoral retreat with trails, trees and wildlife. It is designated by the City of Savannah as a forest preserve and protected from disturbance that would compromise its ecosystems or its natural beauty.

The Savannah Tree Foundation has assumed a stewardship role for the forest, guiding Discovery Walks at various times of the year. You will learn about the various land forms, soil types, tree and plant species, wildlife and ongoing plans for interpretive opportunities. Discovery walkers will see firsthand the hazards of non-native invasives, those species that may appear attractive but which can take over and threaten the health of native plants.

Trails wind through isolated wetlands, mixed hardwood forest, and live oak uplands. Of great interest are topographical variations that create a hilly effect - another surprise in our flat coastal plain. Weather conditions at the time of your visit will affect the size of wetlands areas.

Children will enjoy wandering the extensive trail system. Poison ivy thrives in this forest; use appropriate caution. Once inside the dense forest, visitors will forget how close to home they actually are. During hot summer months, there is a measurable drop in temperature beneath the thick canopies. Be sure to remind young adventurers to stay on the trails and carry out only what they brought in. Old clothes and old shoes are recommended, as there is no pavement in the forest.

The forest is open year round. Currently, the trail system is reached from the parking lot of the Tennis Complex. Turn left upon entering from Skidaway Road and proceed as far as the lot extends. For schedule and other information about Discovery Walks, call the Savannah Tree Foundation, 233-8733.

BETHESDA HOME FOR BOYS

Union Society of Savannah
P.O. Box 13039
Savannah, GA 31499
(912) 351-2040
Located at 9520 Ferguson Ave.

■■■

DAYS/HOURS OF OPERATION
Museum and Office Hours, Monday-Friday, 9 a.m. - 5 p.m.
Nature trail and chapel, sunrise to sunset

ADMISSION
Free; donations accepted

FACILITIES
Parking
Picnic area
Restrooms
Trail
Water fountain

SPECIAL EVENTS
Annual Labor Day festival with arts and crafts, games and rides,
　　food, silent auction, entertainment.

HINTS
* Bug Spray
* Allow 1 hour
* Bring a picnic

*"My favorite part of the visit was seeing the raccoon
climb up and go into the dead Palmetto tree."*

Joe Ratterree, age 10
Tom McKee, Jr., age 10

> ### "My favorite part of the visit was seeing the pecan trees and finding some pecans (October)."
>
> *Billy McKee, age 5*

Listed on the National Register of Historic Places, Bethesda recalls a graceful era uncluttered by the noise of traffic. A traditional brick archway marks the entrance to Bethesda. Visitors then drive down a majestic live-oak-lined lane to a cluster of historic and modern buildings which comprise the Bethesda Home for Boys.

Bethesda's peaceful, pastoral setting on the banks of the Moon River (made famous by Johnny Mercer's song of the same name) is directly opposite historic Wormsloe Plantation. The view from Bethesda today is similar to the view two hundred years before.

Founded in 1740 by George Whitefield and James Habersham as an orphanage, Bethesda was located on a King's Grant of land (500 acres) by the Royal Charter of 1732. The orphanage was relatively self-sufficient, raising its own food through a productive garden and tending livestock. Today, pastures of grazing cows and horses can be seen from Ferguson Avenue or from the nature trail, continuing the tradition begun in 1740.

In 1801, after the establishment of the Savannah Home for Girls, Bethesda limited its residents to boys. Bethesda is managed by the Union Society, a benevolent society established in 1750.

The museum is located in the Burroughs Cottage (1883), Bethesda's oldest remaining building. A tabby brick walk leads the visitor to the Cunningham Historic Center (the museum), filled with portraits, pictures, a model of Bethesda, reading tables, eclectic collections of bones, rocks, tools, bottles and models of ships.

The Whitefield Chapel, located next to Burroughs Cottage, was constructed in 1925 in memory of the founder of Bethesda. Children may want to notice the brick floors in the herringbone pattern, stained glass windows, and moveable wooden pews. A visit to the balcony provides a bird's eye view of both Bethesda and the chapel.

The ½ mile nature trail, opened in May, 1993, begins just behind the office at the base of a magnificent live oak tree. A map with detailed marker-by-marker descriptions is located in a large black mailbox at the start of the trail. Wooden markers along the trail identify primarily trees, as well as scenic vistas and historic sites. Spectacular marsh views, ancient live oaks, and rural pastures are hallmarks of the trail, which is well worth the hike even with young children. There is even a dock on a creek which at high tide holds promise for crabbing, shrimping, and fishing. It would be wise first to seek permission from the office, however, before throwing in a line.

Over the two centuries of Bethesda's existence, more than 8000 children have lived at Bethesda. Currently, Bethesda operates a residential facility and a school for boys who need a structured environment. Programs for the boys at Bethesda allow for growth in the academic, spiritual, and physical areas. An on-campus school was opened in September, 1992. Bethesda means "House of Mercy," and it continues to carry on its mission of mercy into its third century.

CHATHAM COUNTY AQUATIC CENTER

7240 Sallie Mood Drive
Savannah, GA 31406
912-652-6793
www.chathamcounty.org/pwps_aquatic.html

- -

DAYS/HOURS OF OPERATION
Monday through Friday: 6 a.m. to 8 p.m.
Saturday: 7 a.m. to 6 p.m.
Closed Sundays

Summer only:
Monday through Friday, 12 noon to 3:45 p.m.
    and 4:45 to 7:45 p.m.-school sessions for daycare facilities

ADMISSION
Chatham County residents:
$5 per person, 13 and older
$3 children 3 to 12
Children 2 and under free with paid adult
$4 for Seniors 55 and over,
    college students, Active Duty Military
Non county residents add $1 to each fee schedule

Open Swim Punch cards available
Annual and monthly memberships available

FACILITIES
Drink and snack vending machines
50-meter lap pool
Handicapped accessible
Locker rooms handicapped accessible
Recreational pool
Restrooms
Swim Shop
Water fountains

HINTS
* Plan for at least one hour, longer for a group of children
* Take snacks
* Read the Pool Rules carefully

SPECIAL EVENTS
Birthday parties

"You can swim even when it is cold and raining outside."
Katie Ratterree, age 10

The Chatham County Aquatic Center makes swimming a year-round opportunity, with two pools, a large deck and a variety of classes for all ages. This might be the perfect outing during dreary winter months when indoor diversions have been exhausted.

Located on Sallie Mood Drive, the Aquatic Center is one of several recreational facilities funded by the 1996 Olympic Legacy Special Purpose Local Option Sales Tax. A 50-meter lap pool occupying most of the indoor space is strictly for lap swimming, and therefore more suitable for older children. The Recreational Pool is smaller and has both a lap area and a section with a graduated slope, making entry more comfortable for little ones.

The Aquatic Center welcomes parties and special events on Friday evenings and at certain times on Saturdays. These must be scheduled in advance. There is a fee for this service, which includes tables and chairs for up to 30 people. Food is allowed only in designated areas (no glass containers are allowed inside).

Be sure and ask about special swimming instruction for children. Classes are available for children from ages 6 months (with parent or caregiver) to age 15. In addition, there is instruction for children with special needs. The Aquatic Center is popular with parents of home schooled children and also as a destination for traditional school field trips.

Take the plunge all year 'round at the Chatham County Aquatic Center and enjoy splashing good times.

CHATHAM COUNTY GARDEN CENTER AND BOTANICAL GARDENS

Sponsored by Savannah Area Council of Garden Clubs, Inc.
1388 Eisenhower Drive
Savannah, GA 31406
(912) 355-3883

■ ■

DAYS/HOURS OF OPERATION
Farmhouse and Botanical Gardens:
Monday through Friday: 10 a.m. to 2 p.m.

Botanical Gardens only:
Monday through Sunday: 9:30 a.m. to 4:30 p.m.

ADMISSION
Farmhouse and Botanical Gardens:
    $3 adults, $1 children
Botanical Gardens only:
    $2 adults, $1 children
Group tours available

FACILITIES
Garden paths
Handicapped access
Parking
Restrooms
Visitors center

SPECIAL EVENTS
Classes and workshops on gardening, crafts and flower arranging
Seasonal plant sales
Tours of private gardens
Flower shows
Holiday House Tour and Festival of Lights

"It's neat that they are arranging things so that there will always be something in bloom when you go."

Mary Ellen McKee, age 13

For a refreshing escape from the hustle and bustle of the day-to-day routine, a visit to the Garden Center and Botanical Gardens is well worth the time. With fall, winter, spring and summer gardens established, there will be something blooming year 'round.

The site was established on land donated by Chatham County in 1993 and has been developed and planted primarily by volunteers. Many of Savannah's garden clubs have planted a plot, resulting in a variety of habitats, plant materials, color, texture and themes.

A walk through the Botanical Garden is a sensory experience that will delight children. The 10-acre property also contains a wetland area, a pond, hardwood and pine forests and an amphitheatre. Trails through the forested areas have been built by Army and Boy Scout volunteers.

Begin a visit by entering the 1840s farmhouse, which was moved here from another location and has been restored by garden club members. The ground floor is furnished in the period of 1840. If you happen to visit when the farmhouse is closed, you can still enjoy touring the gardens.

Outside, children will want to take off and explore perennial, herb, vegetable, courtyard and shade gardens. A children's garden with stepping stones, a pond and brightly colored flowers is designed especially for the younger set. Benches and covered arbors are located here and there for a rest. A wooded trail shaded by native trees skirts the property and features artifacts found on site. Hats, sunscreen and water are recommended during the summer months.

The Botanical Garden is located near Lake Mayer, Bacon Park and Wormsloe, which adventurers may want to consider when planning a longer outing.

LAKE MAYER PARK

Montgomery Crossroads at Sallie Mood Drive
Savannah, GA 31406
(912) 652-6780
(912) 652-6786
www.chathamcounty.org/pwps_recreationmain.html

DAYS/HOURS OF OPERATION
Fall and Winter: 8 a.m. - 10 p.m.
Spring and Summer: 8 a.m. - 11 p.m.

ADMISSION
Free

FACILITIES
Basketball courts (2)
Boat ramp and dock
Fishing
Handball court
Handicapped access
Parking
Picnic areas (open and covered)
Playground
Restrooms
Shelter
Tennis courts (8)
Track (1.5 miles)
Vending machines

SPECIAL EVENTS
Easter Egg Hunt
Fishing Rodeo
Summer Camp
Family Nature Day
Christmas Camp

HINTS
* Take a picnic
* Bug Spray recommended in spring and fall months
* Good place for beginner fishing
* Take stale bread to feed ducks and geese
* Fun place for birthday parties, family reunions, church picnics
  and other gatherings, Pavilions available for rent.

"When I was 3, my dad brought me here and taught me how to fish."

Joe Ratterree, age 9

"I like to feed bread to the ducks."

Katie Ratterree, age 5

Lake Mayer is a 75-acre county-owned park with enough recreational activities to keep most people busy for hours. It is named for the late Henry Mayer, the Chatham County Commissioner who in the 1950s conceived the idea for this park. Completed in 1972, Lake Mayer Park is encircled by a 35-acre lake stocked with bass, bream, channel catfish, and more. This park is popular year-round, and during the spring and fall months it bustles with people and activities.

If there is any one place in Chatham County where the entire family can have a good time, this is it. Mom and Dad can jog or walk the 1.5 mile track while younger ones bike or skate alongside. There are 8 tennis courts, 2 basketball courts, a handball court, and a playground. Fishing is permitted just about anywhere on the lake, but the area near the picnic tables is a favorite spot for beginners who are almost guaranteed a nibble by some of the little fish. A small can of whole kernel corn will provide more than enough bait for a morning or afternoon of casting.

One of the favorite activities for Lake Mayer visitors is feeding the ducks and geese who live within the park. When the park opened, 15 baby ducklings were introduced. Over the years, especially just after Easter, other ducklings have come to live here, and the population has grown to include mallards and wood ducks. There are also geese and seagulls in huge flocks. During the early spring months ducks and geese are nesting, and a few weeks later flocks of babies waddle around after their mothers. Whatever the variety or size of winged animal, they are all hungry and enjoy eating bread crumbs and crackers. A mild word of caution - hungry geese can be rather aggressive, and some are actually taller than small toddlers.

The jogging trail which includes exercise stations, is frequented at all hours, with heavier use in late afternoon and early evening. The path is well-lighted. Classes in boating, sailing, karate, arts and crafts, and other activities are available during the year. There are several annual festivals and events held here, also. The pavilions can be rented for private use.

SKIDAWAY ISLAND STATE PARK

Managed by The Georgia Department of Natural Resources
52 Diamond Causeway
Skidaway Island
Savannah, GA 31411
(912) 598-2300, 598-2301
http//:gastateparks.org/info/skidaway

■ ■

DAYS/HOURS OF OPERATION
Daily: 7 a.m. - 10 p.m.
Park office hours: 8 a.m. - 5 p.m.

ADMISSION
$3 per car

FACILITIES
Camping
Food/drink machines
Handicapped access
Parking
Pets on leash
Phone
Picnic areas
Restrooms
Shelters
Swimming pool,
   Memorial Day to Labor Day
Trails
Visitors Center

SPECIAL EVENTS
Please contact the park to find out
   about upcoming events

HINTS

* For fall, spring, or summer visits, bring bug spray
* Bring a picnic lunch, particularly drinks
* Good place for bike riding
* Bring stroller or baby carrier for young children
* Allow 2 to 3 hours
* Bring binoculars
* Guided hikes available with advance reservations
* Shelters can be reserved for parties. Playgrounds, trails, camp ground, and lots of picnic tables foster many party possibilities

"My favorite part was the playground, particularly the tire swing."

Tom McKee, Jr., age 10

"I liked walking on the trails."

Jessica Konter, age 12

"I liked seeing the wildlife and the marsh."

Mary Ellen McKee, age 13

Skidaway Island State Park encompasses 533 acres including large expanses of salt marsh, freshwater wetlands, and mixed pine/hardwood forest. This is the only state park in Chatham County with camping facilities (88 tent and trailer sites), plus it boasts a Junior Olympic Swimming Pool, five large picnic areas with shelters, playgrounds, and an amphitheater.

The park, located on the inland edge of Skidaway Island, is accessible by car. Of historic interest, the park contains two large Confederate earthworks which were built to protect the Skidaway Narrows.

There are two trails within the park and guided trail hikes are available with advance reservations. The Big Ferry Nature Trail is three miles long and takes approximately an hour and half to hike at a relaxed pace. Winding through the woods, over wetlands, and skirting the salt marsh, this trail has side trips to an old moonshine still and the Confederate earthworks.

Educational markers along the trail point out natural, archeological, and historical highlights.

There is an Indian shell midden from the late Archaic period which shows human activity from two thousand years ago. Even the earliest Americans liked to eat oysters!

The other trail, the Sandpiper Trail, begins behind the visitor's center. It is a mile long and takes approximately twenty minutes to hike. The trail guide coordinates trail markers with questions and answers along the way, and visitors on this trail have one of the best opportunities to observe the salt marsh up-close. Fiddler crabs scurry away in huge armies as children approach. Depending on the season, a marsh hawk, osprey, or red-tailed hawk may be spotted. The impressionable marsh mud always holds tracks of raccoons, deer, or wading birds. A look-out tower, a favorite with children, provides a birds-eye view of the large expanse of marsh.

There is plenty to do here for a day-long family outing, a church picnic, or a school field trip. Advance reservations for groups are recommended because Skidaway Island State Park is a popular destination for many.

WORMSLOE HISTORIC SITE

7601 Skidaway Road
Savannah, GA 31406
(912) 353-3023
www.wormsloe.org

- -

DAYS/HOURS OF OPERATION
Tuesday-Saturday: 9 a.m. - 5 p.m.
Sunday: 2 p.m. - 5:30 p.m.
Closed Monday, except legal holidays
Closed Thanksgiving, Christmas, and New Year's Day

ADMISSION
$4 per adult/$3.50 per senior citizen
$1 per child under 18 / $2.50 age 6-18 / under 6 free
$3.00 per adult for tour groups (15 or more)
$2.00 per person for youth groups (15 or more)
(Bus drivers and group leaders free)

FACILITIES
Audio-visual presentation
Brochures
Drink machines
Gift Shop
Handicapped access in museum; wheelchair access in museum and
    along wide trail; wheelchair available on site; prior arrangements
    can be made for vehicular transport of handicapped people.
Museum
Parking
Picnic area
Restrooms

HINTS
* Allow 1 hour minimum
* Great place for children to run around
* Bug spray advisable in warm seasons
* Advance reservations required for large groups

> **"I like the trails through the woods. We went here with my cub scouts. This is a great place to go with friends."**
>
> *Joe Ratterree, age 9*

One of the most breathtaking vistas in the lowcountry is the one and a half mile drive into Wormsloe under the magnificent canopy of live oaks. These trees were planted in 1892-1893 to honor the birth of a descendant of Wormsloe's original owner, Noble Jones. The gates at the entrance of the drive were added when this same descendant turned twenty-one.

In 1736, three years after the colony of Georgia was established at Savannah, founder James Edward Oglethorpe dispatched fellow colonist Noble Jones to a site south of town near a bend in the Skidaway River. Jones' mission was to build a fortified colonial outpost to protect the new settlement from attack by the Spanish in Florida. Fortunately, the colonists

never encountered the Spanish in local waters. The 800-plus acres of land known as Wormsloe (the name possibly derived from a Welch name meaning "dragon's lair") remained in the hands of Jones' descendants until 1973, when most of the property was sold to the State of Georgia via The Nature Conservancy to be operated as a historic site. All that remains of the fortified house built by Jones and his men is the tabby foundation of the house and much of the surrounding walls, but a beautifully made, scale model of the house is on display for visitors.

The first stop after the parking lot is the museum where the office, small auditorium, and a gallery of exhibits are located. Restrooms and a vending machine are reached through a different entrance. A seventeen-minute audio-visual overview of the site is shown frequently and highly recommended. Following that, visitors enter the exhibit area through iron gates designed for the museum by well-known ironsmith Ivan Bailey. Well-labeled wall maps, artifact displays, and scale models of Jones' house, Fort Frederica, a Spanish fort, and an Indian village all assist in interpreting the coastal fortification system of colonial days. Site rangers are available to answer questions.

After leaving the museum building, there are two paths from which to choose, each ending at the site of Mr. Jones' first house. The wide path is the most direct, but the interpretive nature trail, slightly longer, is more intriguing. The latter wanders through the woods and around beautiful views of the marsh and river through moss-laden trees. Just off the path is a clearing featuring a small wooden structure and a corral. This area is used for living history demonstrations for groups and special occasions. The small house is an example of wattle and daub (or in 20th century words, mud and sticks) construction. Every effort should be made to visit Wormsloe during one of these demonstrations when people dress in colonial garb and act out a day in the life of colonial Georgia.

The path eventually opens onto a cleared area revealing the tabby foundation and surrounding walls of Mr. Jones' house. Tabby, a mixture of sand, oyster shell and lime, was the colonial equivalent of cement, and suitable for structures built near the water. The tabby foundation and walls here are one of the oldest remaining structures from Oglethorpe's time. A little imagination and common sense will assist children in figuring out the basic floor plan of this early Georgia home.

After passing the tabby ruins, explorers will come to a gravestone which was placed to commemorate the family of Noble Jones, buried on the site. Both the wide trail and the interpretive nature trail lead back toward the museum and parking area.

Wormsloe now has a 10K (6 mile) walking tour approved for the Happy Wanderers Club. A brochure with details is available at the museum.

FOR CHILDREN OVER 12

∎∎

(ALL LOCATED IN HISTORIC DISTRICT)

1. Andrew Low House
2. Flannery O'Connor House
3. Green Meldrim House
4. Isaiah Davenport House
5. Owens-Thomas House

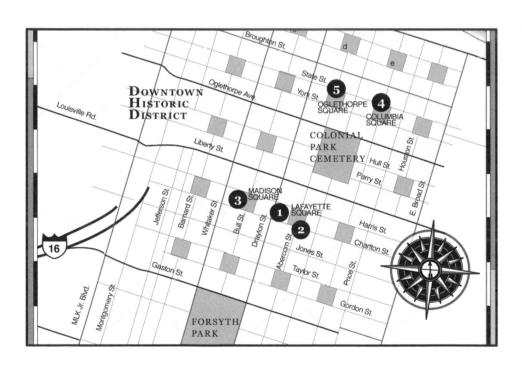

ANDREW LOW HOUSE

Headquarters of The National Society of
  The Colonial Dames of America in the State of Georgia
329 Abercorn Street
Savannah, GA 31401
(912) 233-6854

■ ■

DAYS/HOURS OF OPERATION
Weekdays: 10 a.m. - 4:30 p.m. (Last tour begins at 4 p.m.)
Sundays: Noon - 4:30 p.m.
Closed Thursdays, and National Holidays

ADMISSION
$7.50 per adult
$4.50 per child, Girl Scouts, students with ID
Under six is free
Tour Groups $4.50 per person

FACILITIES
Gift Shop
25-minute video presentation

> "The old glass bookcase panes were fascinating. To
> think of glass as a liquid just baffles me!"
>
> *Thomas Beason, age 12*

The sophisticated Andrew Low House, circa 1848, combines European elegance with West Indian plantation influence. Andrew Low's famous daughter-in-law, Juliette Gordon Low, lived here from 1886 until 1927. For Girl Scouts everywhere, this house deserves a pilgrimage. In the morning room in the front of the house, Juliette Gordon Low signed the original charter to found the Girl Scouts in 1912. It was also in an upstairs bedroom that the founder of the Girl Scouts died in 1927.

Facing Lafayette Square, the house was designed by architect John Norris of New York for the wealthy cotton merchant, Andrew Low.

Andrew Low came from Scotland to Savannah to become a cotton exporter, but he maintained a baronial castle in England and spent only his winters in Savannah. It was Andrew's son, William, who married Juliette Gordon Low.

Is glass a liquid or a solid? Surprisingly enough, it is a liquid! Children will be interested to see old glass panes in the bookcase of the morning room which are slowly dripping downward, thinning at the top. The house is furnished in period antiques and during the time of Andrew Low there were over fifteen servants managing this household.

Two historic figures were guests in this house. Southern General Robert E. Lee stayed here in 1870, and he had the honor of being named the godfather of Andrew Low's youngest daughter. Also, William Makepeace Thackeray, author of *Vanity Fair*, stayed here in 1853 and 1856 when he was on lecture tours in the United States.

The formal dining room is grandly furnished and hails from another era when the children dined downstairs in the children's dining room. Children were not allowed to dine with the adults until they learned proper etiquette!

Another point of interest is the dry moat which surrounds the house outside. This dry moat followed a European design and was used as a passageway for the servants navigating outside the house.

Majestic, but frowning lions grace the entryway to the house. The expressions on the lions' faces denote pussycats rather than fierce lions, and it is said that Juliette Gordon Low patted the lions on the head as she entered and left the house.

The Colonial Dames of Georgia maintain the house in keeping with its noble past. It is well worth a visit, and older children and Girl Scouts will enjoy this glimpse into sophisticated 19th century life. Well-informed guides provide entertaining, anecdotal, and historical information.

FLANNERY O'CONNOR HOUSE

Owned and Managed by The Flannery O'Connor Home
    Foundation, Inc.
207 East Charlton Street
Savannah, GA 31401
(912) 233-6014
www.flanneryoconnorhome.org

■■ ■■

DAYS/HOURS OF OPERATION
Friday, Saturday, Sunday
1 p.m. - 4 p.m.

ADMISSION
Donations Accepted

SPECIAL EVENTS
Special Sunday programs, such as readings, guest lectures, films,
    or seminars.

> "This house is recommended for someone who has
> read her work and knows who she is."
>
> *Mary Ellen McKee, age 13*

Located on quiet Lafayette Square, the newly renovated childhood home of Southern novelist Flannery O'Connor is a modest four-story stucco house. A historical marker is located in front of the house with a brief history of Flannery O'Connor who died in 1964 at the early age of 39.

Flannery O'Connor spent the first thirteen years of her life here in this house and around Lafayette Square. She attended the Cathedral and Catholic school on the square, and the faith and symbols of Catholicism play an important role in her short stories and novels.

The house was purchased in 1989 by the O'Connor Home Foundation. Furnishings include actual pieces owned and used by O'Connor's family, as well as other period items.

Flannery O'Connor stands beside William Faulkner, Eudora Welty, and Walker Percy as a distinguished Southern writer. She won the O'Henry Award for the best short story of the year on three separate occasions and a collection of her short stories won the National Book Award in 1972. As a child in the O'Connor home, she helped raise ducks and chickens in the courtyard and even taught a chicken to walk backwards. Notecards bearing the design of the house are sold inside.

GREEN-MELDRIM HOUSE

14 West Macon Street
On Madison Square
Savannah, GA 31401
(912) 233-3845

■ ■

DAYS/HOURS OF OPERATION
Tuesday, Thursday, Friday, Saturday: 10 a.m. - 4 p.m.
Closed December 15 through January 15 and
  two weeks prior to Easter

ADMISSION
$5 adults
$2 students

FACILITIES
Restrooms

HINTS
* Combine with a Madison Square outing

> ## "This place fits in with what I am
> ## studying in school."
>
> *Recent visitor, age 13*

The Green-Meldrim House was completed in 1853 as the residence of Charles Green. This Gothic revival-style house was designed by John Norris, a New York architect who also designed Massie School, the United States Custom House, and the Andrew Low Mansion. In 1892, the house was bought by Judge Peter Meldrim, and in 1943, St. John's Episcopal Church purchased it for use as a parish house.

In addition to its architectural and historical significance, the Green-Meldrim House is well known as the house used by Union General William

Tecumseh Sherman as headquarters in 1864, at the end of his March to the Sea. Owner Charles Green gave up most of the house to the General and his troops. Shortly after moving in, General Sherman sent a telegram to Abraham Lincoln, offering the city of Savannah to him as a Christmas present. Charles Green's hospitality may have prevented Savannah from the total destruction that Sherman inflicted upon other southern towns along his route.

The grandeur of this house is evident from the moment visitors approach. Entry to the house is through three sets of doors. The massive outer doors, almost intimidating, are compatible with the gothic style of the house. Inside, the rooms are spacious and cool, with high ceilings and tiled floors. Much of the interior door hardware is silver-plated. Elaborate crown moldings, marble mantles, and enormous chandeliers reflect the elegance of the home.

Visitors will enjoy a guided tour which takes between 30 and 40 minutes. Docents will point out furnishings and other details significant to the history of the house. After touring the house, visitors will want to view the garden and wading pool.

ISAIAH DAVENPORT HOUSE

A property of the Historic Savannah Foundation
324 East State Street
Savannah, GA 31401
(912) 236-8097
www.davenporthousemuseum.org

■ ■

DAYS/HOURS OF OPERATION
Monday-Saturday: 10 a.m. - 4 p.m.
Sunday: 1 p.m. - 4 p.m.
Closed Major Holidays

ADMISSION
$8 per adult
$5 per child (7 - 18 years)
Children 6 and under, free
Museum Shop and Garden, No charge

HINTS
* Tours are given on the hour and half hour
* Last tour begins at 4 p.m.

*"A lot of old-timey details that you have to notice,
like the plaster work or designs and the pictures
on the wall, make this a neat house."*

Mary Ellen McKee, age 13

Located on charming Columbia Square, the Davenport House is an elegant reminder of the past. Completed in 1820 by master builder Isaiah Davenport, the house is a classic example of Federal architecture. During the early and mid-1900s, the historic home had become a tenement, the floors divided into separate apartments. In 1955, the house was scheduled to be demolished to make way for a parking lot. Fortunately, seven Savannah ladies raised the $22,500 to purchase the home and save it from the wrecking ball. This was the founding act of the Historic Savannah Foundation.

Today, many visitors enjoy this architectural and historical treasure. The Davenport House has two exhibit floors open for guided tours, as well as the outdoor garden. The gift shop carries many items unique to Savannah, as well as reproductions that may have been used in Isaiah Davenport's time period. Period furniture and accoutrements which decorate the house, the period feel and architectural details in the rooms and on the stairways, doorways and around the windows make the Davenport House worth a visit.

OWENS-THOMAS HOUSE

Owned by the Telfair Museum of Art
124 Abercorn Street
Savannah, GA 31401
(912) 233-9743
www.telfair.org

DAYS/HOURS OF OPERATION
Tuesday-Saturday: 10 a.m. - 5 p.m.
Sunday: 1 - 5 p.m.
Monday: 12 p.m. - 5 p.m.
(Last tour begins at 4:30)

ADMISSION
Telfair members free
$10 per adult
$4 per student K-12
$5 per college student
$25 per family (2 adults, 2 children)
$30 per family for all three Telfair sites (2 adults, 2 children)
$15 per adult for all three Telfair sites
Children under 5 free
Discounts for AAA and military

FACILITIES
Gift Shop

HINTS
* Allow 45 minutes to 1 hour
* Ask about the children's activity sheet, "Can You Find It"

> ### "I've never seen such a big dining room table. A lot of people must have lived in this house."
> *Katie Ratterree, age 5*

> ### "It's neat to have a bridge inside a house."
> *Joe Ratterree, age 10*

The Owens-Thomas House is one of America's finest examples of the English Regency style of architecture. Like the Telfair Museum, it was designed by English architect, William Jay. This house was built in 1819 for cotton merchant and banker Richard Richardson, and is a good representation of the house of a prominent, wealthy Savannahian at the time. Unfortunately, Mr. Richardson lived here only three years before bankruptcy. Afterwards, the house was run as a lodging house for several years. In 1825, the Revolutionary War hero, the Marquis de Lafayette, stayed here as a guest, and is said to have delivered a speech from the cast iron balcony overlooking President Street. The house was purchased by the Owens family in 1830. In 1951, an Owens descendant, Miss Margaret Thomas, left the house to the Telfair to be operated as a house museum.

Admission is purchased and visits begin in the carriage house behind the main building, reached from President Street. The gift shop is located in the original carriage house and hay loft. The other part of the building, the original location of the slave quarters, now is used as the Orientation gallery for the entire site. Here also is an exhibit from the Acacia Collection of African Americana.

Throughout the house one can appreciate the architect's fondness for symmetry and for the forms and shapes found in ancient classical buildings. Columns, gentle curves and ellipses and the Greek key design are some of the reminders of the classical tradition. After entering the house, visitors begin a docent-guided tour that takes about 30 minutes. Fidgety youngsters may prefer to chase butterflies in the garden (with Mom or Dad, of course).

The house is made of tabby, a mixture of lime, oyster shells and sand, and covered with stucco. An exposed area on the southern side of the house shows what tabby looks like. Inside, there are several unusual design features. The decorative corners of the drawing room make the ceiling appear rounded. In the dining room, there are curved walls and doors, and an interestingly lit window with amber glass panes providing a soft glow.

Upstairs, there is a bridge connecting the front and back of the house. The balcony facing south is one of the earliest uses of cast iron in architecture in Savannah.

The garden is known as a *par terre* garden, referring to its symmetrical division into bordered beds. Children enjoy wandering its stone paths.

This house is one of the stops on Massie Heritage Center's "Breaking the Bonds" tour for children. The visit here includes the slave quarters, the basement of the main house and its parlor level floor. Contact Massie Center for more information.

MIDWAY

1. Fort Morris State Historic Site
2. LeConte-Woodmanston Rice Plantation and Botanical Garden
3. Melon Bluff Center / Palmyra Plantation
4. Midway Church and Museum
5. Seabrook Village

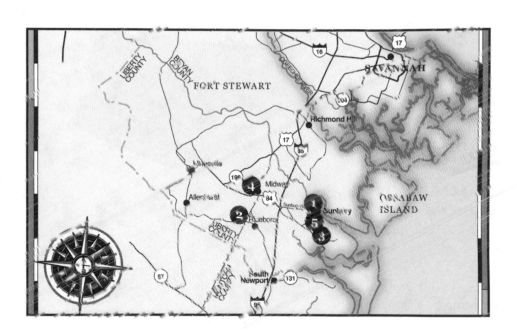

FORT MORRIS STATE HISTORIC SITE

Route 1, Box 236
2559 Fort Morris Rd.
Midway, Georgia 31320
(912) 884-5999
www.gastateparks.org

■ ■

DAYS/HOURS OF OPERATION
Tuesday - Saturday: 9 a.m. to 5 p.m.
Sundays: 9:30 a.m. to 5:30 p.m.

ADMISSION
$3 adults, $2.50 Seniors, $1.50 youth (6 to 18 yrs)
Groups of 15 or more receive a $.50 discount per person

FACILITIES
Museum
Nature Trail
Picnic Area
Pioneer and primitive camping
Restrooms
Sea kayaking trail

SPECIAL EVENTS
Reenactments and holiday celebrations in
February, April, June, October and December

HINTS
• Living history guided tour requires 2-week notice
• Bring bug spray, hats, water, snacks
• Allow 1 ½ hours

> "This is a perfect place for me because I like
> boating and it has a boating ramp."
> *Darr Smith, age 9*

> "It's fun because there are lots of places to exercise."
> *Ansley Guthrie, age 9*

Four miles east of the I-95 Midway exit, take a left on Trade Hill Road which dead-ends at Fort Morris Road. The entrance to the fort is 2 miles ahead on the right.

Fort Morris, originally a Guale Indian Village, was built shortly after the Continental Congress convened in 1776. Situated on a low bluff on the Medway River, the 70-acre Fort Morris was built to defend the thriving port of Sunbury. The town of Sunbury, founded in 1758, had disappeared by the early 19th century. The Revolutionary War, two hurricanes, and a change in crops shifted the residents elsewhere. All that remain of the town today are Fort Morris and the Sunbury cemetery.

Fort Morris is a lovely spot for a picnic overlooking the marsh. Begin your tour at the small museum with an 11-minute film on Sunbury. Then, pick up a self-guided walking tour and enjoy a leisurely stroll around this historic site.

Marsh views, ancient live oak trees, earthenwork fortifications and an incredible view of St. Catherine's Sound out to the Atlantic Ocean are part of the path around the fort and the short nature trail.

Fort Morris has the only Revolutionary War earthworks remaining in Georgia. Fort Morris was renamed Fort King George after it was captured by the British. During the War of 1812, it was named yet again; this time it became Fort Defiance. With this much history, there are several special events that might decide when you visit. Call ahead to find out about the different events planned in February, April, June, October, and December.

LECONTE-WOODMANSTON RICE PLANTATION AND BOTANICAL GARDEN

P. O. Box 179
Midway, GA 31320
(912) 884-6500

DAYS/HOURS OF OPERATION
Tuesday, Wednesday, Friday: 10 a.m. to 3 p.m.

ADMISSION
$2 donation per person
Group rates available

FACILITIES
Parking
Picnic Tables
Restrooms
Trail

HINTS
* Visit in fall, winter, or spring
* Allow two hours for visit plus an hour driving time
* Call ahead for directions and to alert manager of your visit
* Bring a picnic, drinks, and bug spray

"The trail is cool around the old rice field."
Billy McKee, age 12

Getting to LeConte-Woodmanston Plantation is an adventure in itself. Historic signs mark the way to LeConte, which is part of the historic Liberty Trail.

Before bridges and modern highways entered our landscape, ferries, rivers and old Indian trails were the main modes of transportation. LeConte-Woodmanston Plantation was located on the old Barrington Ferry Road, an active thoroughfare in the 18th century. As you wind down small black-top country roads that turn into dirt roads with no gas stations or hamburger stops, LeConte-Woodmanston emerges as a reminder of life before cars.

LeConte Plantation was founded in 1760, by the grandsons of a French Huguenot immigrant who settled in coastal Georgia. The LeConte-Woodmanston site was added to the National Register of Historic Places in 1973. This rice plantation was strategically located just six miles from an old colonial fort, Fort Barrington, and close to the thriving Midway community which produced two signers of the Declaration of Independence. Bulltown Swamp bordered the LeConte Plantation which provided fresh water and irrigation for the rice fields.

In 1813, Louis LeConte developed a botanical garden on this site that became internationally known. The garden reached its peak in 1838. One of Louis LeConte's sons helped found the Sierra Club.

Children will enjoy hiking the 20-minute trail which completely encircles one old rice field. The site is completely outdoor oriented, with lots of room to run and play. Look for cypress trees, deer, and armadillos!

No house remains on this old plantation, but the LeConte-Woodmanston Foundation is recreating the gardens and support structures that once were home to an active rice plantation in the 18th century. The farm was active until around 1850.

Originally a 3300 acre plantation, LeConte now is comprised of 60 acres which includes the site of the original home and gardens. Garden clubs, volunteers, and the LeConte-Woodmanston Foundation are working together to re-create the landscape of the original working farm. A barn, cabin, formal gardens, and a 20-minute trail around an old rice field are the main attractions.

The gardens have unusual and historic plantings, such as an arc of double-white camellias (*Alba plena*) which were one of LeConte's favorites, and a *Franklinea Altamaha*, a rare tree from the bay tree family named for Benjamin Franklin. Quince, hydrangeas, roses, a turks turban, blueberries, scuppernong grapes, an old cabbage palm, and a Confederate rose can also be found. Story boards are located along the paths which provide visuals and historic details about the site. The Site Director will also provide a tour, with advanced notice.

MELON BLUFF NATURE CENTER AND PALMYRA PLANTATION & BARN

2999 Islands Highway
Midway, GA 31320
(912) 884-5779 or (888) 246-8188
www.melonbluff.net

DAYS/HOURS OF OPERATION
Saturday: 9 a.m. to 4 p.m. or by appointment.
Closed, 3rd week of May until Labor Day.

ADMISSION
$3 per day. Children under 6 free.

FACILITIES
Gift Shop
Interpretative Programs
Horse Trails
Parking
Picnic Area
Restrooms
Self-touring trails
Shelter
Trails with guided tours

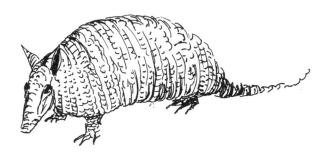

HINTS
*Bring bug spray, water, snacks
*Catering is possible for groups
*Pre-arrange for visits other than on Saturday
*Allow 3 to 4 hours

"The best part was when I fed the ox and the goats,
walking by the water, and seeing the camellias."

Ke'ambra Pinckney, age 10

As a destination all by itself or as part of your day-trek to Liberty County, consider a stop at the Melon Bluff Nature Center, which is not far from Fort Morris. Just 3.2 miles east of I-95, the Nature Center is a rustic building located on the south side of the highway. The parking area is just past the green-and-white Melon Bluff mailbox.

The Nature Center has a gift shop and lots of information about Melon Bluff, which is the hub for 25 miles of biking and hiking trails. If your children like to mountain bike, this is an ideal place to let them loose.

Melon Bluff Plantation is a privately-owned nature preserve in Midway that represents one family's commitment to the unspoiled landscape of the coastal area. Managed by landowner Laura Devendorf and daughter Meredith, Melon Bluff was voted by Atlanta Magazine as "the best alternative to development on the coast."

Dramatically "underbuilt," this is life on the coast the way nature intended. Come prepared with insect repellent, hats, protective clothing, and good walking shoes to enjoy the 3,000 acres of hiking and biking trails.

Melon Bluff is a place that demands repeat visits. There is far too much to explore in one day. Group tours, kayak rides and special events are always possible. The owners know how to keep groups of lively children focused and busy. For an unusual birthday party, Melon Bluff's outdoor possibilities are fascinating, particularly a wagon ride for the children. Meredith Devendorf will custom-design an unforgettable morning or afternoon event that might include a game of Money in the Haystack, swimming in the pool house, nature scavenger hunts, or a ride in the covered wagon drawn by mules Kit and Kate.

The Tree-House Trail at Melon Bluff is interactive, winding through wetlands, then up 26 feet through a sandhill community, then through a maritime forest. At the top of the hill is a treehouse that looks out over cypress trees and marsh. The entire trail is less than a mile.

Palmyra Plantation, a little farther down the road on the north side of Islands Highway, is a piece of paradise waiting for explorers. By appointment only, Palmyra offers special events such as moonlight hay rides, farm tours, garden (camellia) walks, and kayaking trips. Special events are posted on the web site. Catering is also available for special events. Overnight stays at Palmyra's luxurious bed and breakfast can be arranged. Advance reservations are necessary.

These two sites encompass thousands of acres of wetlands, mature hardwood forests, saltwater marshes, cypress swamps, freshwater ponds, salt water creeks, and live oak trees hundreds of years old. Relax and enjoy.

MIDWAY CHURCH AND MUSEUM

U.S. Highway 17 South
P.O. Box 195
Midway, Georgia 31320
(912) 884-5837
www.themidwaymuseum.org

- -

DAYS/HOURS OF OPERATION
Tuesday-Saturday: 10 a.m. to 4 p.m.
Sunday: 2 p.m. to 4 p.m.
Guided tours available

ADMISSION
$5 per adult, $4 per senior citizen, $2 children
Discounts available for groups

FACILITIES
Gift shop
Handicapped Access
Museum
Parking
Picnic tables
Restrooms

HINTS
* Allow 45 minutes
* Graveyard tour available with advanced notice.
* Docents dress in period costumes.
* Special events include a Halloween event

"The coolest part was the lady playing the glasses."
Billy McKee, Age 12

Driving south from Savannah on I-95, take Exit 87 (the second Richmond Hill exit) and follow U.S. 17 South. After a 10-minute drive, a sign announces the Midway Museum and Church, 1 mile. The museum is first, on the left, with a small parking area, beautiful live oaks and picnic tables. The church is next to the museum.

Although house museums are not always easy with children, this one works for several reasons. Be sure to accept the offer for a tour, which is full of stories and interesting tidbits of historical information.

In the front room are Midway's famous musical glasses, which are played by dipping a finger in vinegar and rubbing the rims of the glasses. The sound is startlingly beautiful, and children will be fascinated by the clear, ringing sound made by what looks like ordinary drinking glasses. An innocent-looking walking cane converts to a 19th century concealed gun, perhaps a James Bond predecessor!

The tour also gives an overview of Georgia history, including the Revolutionary War and the Civil War, both of which touched coastal Liberty County. Midway and Sunbury were very influential during Georgia's early days.

Outside the house museum is a detached kitchen and a huge salt vat used to make animal salt licks from seawater. Children will enjoy using the impressive, large brass key to open the front door of the old Midway church next door. The key is obtained in the museum gift shop.

Because of this county's strong revolutionary support - it was named Liberty County for a reason! - the Midway church was burned by British troops in 1778. The church standing today was built in 1792, and was occupied by part of General Sherman's army in December, 1864.

The last weekend in October, just before Halloween, docents hold a special program called "Tales and Legends of the Cemetery." A visit to Midway Church and Museum is a fun history lesson as a trip back into time.

WORD SEARCH

Midway Museum
Live Oaks
Revolutionary War
Salt Vat
Church
Music
Musical Glasses
Civil War
Liberty County
Gwinnett
Key

```
E M T E A A S D V C J F L E Q B M E O F
E U R A T H H I B D E R J O U M O K M K
A S T B F I E N G L M Y G E I S Y C S P
M I D W A Y M U S E U M D P K P I I O J
B C R T R A M F O A S C Y H S N D V A T
B A W K U N A T D L I V E O A K S I A L
K L R A N U N A T A C D M A V T G L V Q
O G N E R E V O L U T I O N A R Y W A R
R L T S O A T C H E E S E T P C O A N S
V A N U R E A R T A R H L F C H U R C H
L S A L T V A T U R A M S L A D D V R E
C S C A E G G O E T R A I N S T O L I U
K E A Y W I W P T H O N M T L O M I N S
X S R G Y L I B E R T Y C O U N T Y L I
M Q C R E H N B P C S L Y R D L E Y R T
D W K J N O N F H R M K B E O K N D E A
T E M L O K E E P K S B F L K M N Z X F
C B U C A N T O N S G U S N M T U L X G
K R S T L J T R O U K R E I N G F X C K
```

SEABROOK VILLAGE

660 Tradehill Road
Midway, GA 31320
(912) 884-7008

- -

DAYS/HOURS OF OPERATION
Tuesday to Saturday: 10 a.m. to 4 p.m.
Call ahead to verify

ADMISSION
Donations requested. Suggested donation, $8 to $10
Senior Citizens, $6
Group Rate Available

FACILITIES
Picnic Area
Restrooms

HINTS
- Allow two hours
- Great for groups looking for hands-on activities

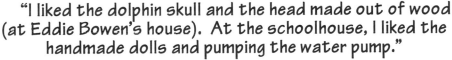

*"I liked the dolphin skull and the head made out of wood
(at Eddie Bowen's house). At the schoolhouse, I liked the
handmade dolls and pumping the water pump."*
Ke'ambra Pinckney, age 10

Seabrook Village is a window into African-American history from 1865
to 1930. Visitors participate in a unique, African-American culture that is
preserved in this living history museum located outside of Midway. The
104-acre site is composed of several cottages, a one-room schoolhouse, a
depot, and a farm.

The best way to see Seabrook is with a group tour, which lasts three
hours. Tours are interactive and can include full meals and entertainment.
One-hour guided tours are also available as well as self-guided tours. Tours

are led by interpreters from families who have been connected to Seabrook Village for over 150 years. If a tour is scheduled in advance, docents will conduct tours in costume.

Pre-arranged activities for children include grinding grits, scarecrow building, planting a garden, clothes-washing on a washboard, cane grinding and syrup boils, and making butter. Old-fashioned games are a favorite for birthday parties, as well as broom-making and wagon rides.

Your tour will probably begin at Eddie Bowen's house, where the office and small museum are located. Eddie Bowen was a root healer and lived here in the 1900s. In the museum is a real bottle-tree, bare branches ornamented with upside-down, brightly colored bottles on each tree-branch. The bottles would capture the evil spirits and protect the house. Other artifacts from the early 1900s include washboards, a peanut roaster, a corn shuck mop, brooms made of broom sage, and a lampshade made of popsicle sticks.

A mile away is the rest of Seabrook Village with its authentic one-room schoolhouse. The school was built in 1875 with boards in the front painted black---the "blackboard." The school was active until the 1950s. Grades 1 through 7 all met together here.

After visiting the schoolhouse, children will enjoy taking turns pumping the water pump. The sulphur-smelling water comes straight from the underground aquifer.

Past the water pump is Eli Gibbons house, built in 1891. Preserved just as it was when the Gibbons lived there, visitors will feel that the original residents might walk through the door at any moment.

Seabrook Village is managed by the Seabrook Village Foundation, a non-profit group. Your visit will help support the work of the Foundation.

CHECK YOUR READING SKILLS

1. **How many acres are in Seabrook Village?**_____

2. **What does a bottle tree do?**_____

3. **Why was a blackboard called a blackboard?**_____

_____

4. **What does the water from the aquifer smell like?**

_____

DARIEN

1. Altamaha Waterfowl Management Area
2. Fort King George Historic Site
3. Harris Neck National Wildlife Refuge
4. Hofwyl-Broadfield Plantation Historic Site
5. Sapelo Island

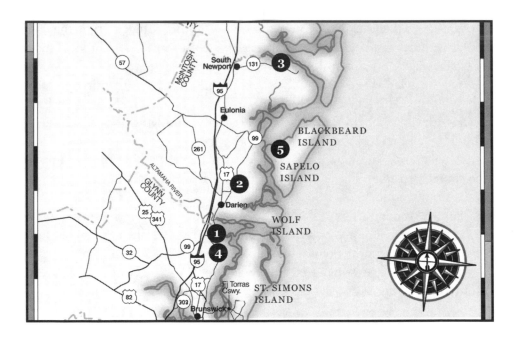

ALTAMAHA WATERFOWL MANAGEMENT AREA

Owned and managed by the
   Georgia Department of Natural Resources, Wildlife Resources Division,
   Game Management
1 Conservation Way, Suite 211
Brunswick, GA 31520
(912) 262-3173
Location: U.S. Highway 17, just south of Darien
Location phone: (912) 437-4569 (not staffed on a regular basis)
www.gohuntgeorgia.com

■ ■

DAYS/HOURS OF OPERATION
Sunup to sundown, year-round

ADMISSION
Free

FACILITIES
Look-out stations for viewing wildlife
Nature trails

HINTS
* Bring bug spray, water to drink, hat, walking stick, binoculars,
  good walking shoes.
* Allow an hour or more, depending on your hiking enthusiasm.
* Controlled hunting is allowed according to DNR regulations.
* September through March are best for viewing wildlife.

"I like being around water."
Ansley Guthrie, age 9

"I like hunting, fishing, boating, animals and the water."
Darr Smith, age 9

Heading south from Darien, just across the bridge over the Butler River,
stands a tall brick tower, the remnant of an old grist mill. Behind the old

grist mill is a 1920s plantation-style house built on the site of the original Butler Plantation. This is Butler Island.

Turn in at the grist mill and house for a short hike on the stretch of the old Highway 17 Bridge which is closed to four-wheel traffic and available to pedestrians and cyclists. Concrete picnic tables dot this stretch of old bridge.

A historic plaque marks the return of Pierce Butler and his daughter, Frances, in 1866 to Butler Island. After her father died, Frances continued to manage the plantation, documented in her book, *Ten Years On a Georgia Plantation*. Offices for the Nature Conservancy's Altamaha River Bioreserve now utilize the 1920s house built by Col. Houston who owned the New York Yankees. It is said that Babe Ruth once visited here!

A small boat landing near the house offers launching for kayaks or canoes. The old rice fields are now managed for wildlife. In the winter months, ducks and hawks are plentiful. During the spring and summer, watch out for snakes and alligators.

Numerous hiking trails and wildlife viewing platforms are on both sides of the road. You could spend several hours here or fifteen minutes, depending on weather and your children's adventurous spirit. But, do come prepared with snacks and water. There are no public facilities, so Darien, just across the river, would provide the nearest restrooms and food.

ACROSS
1. **Famous Baseball Player**
3. **Name of Island**
5. **Reptile**
7. **Nearby town**
9. **Swimming bird**

DOWN
2. **Place to mill rice**
4. **Butler's Daughter**
6. **Indian boat**
8. **Owned the New York Yankees**
10. **Large farm in South**

FORT KING GEORGE HISTORIC SITE

Owned and managed by the Georgia Department of Natural
  Resources, State Parks & Historic Sites Division
1600 Wayne Street
Darien, GA 31405
(912) 437-4770   (912) 437-5479 Fax
www.gastateparks.org/info/ftkinggeorge/

DAYS/HOURS OF OPERATION
Tuesday - Saturday: 9 a.m. - 5 p.m.
Sunday: 2 p.m. - 5:30 p.m.
Closed Monday except for federal holidays, Thanksgiving,
  Christmas and New Year's

ADMISSION
$5 per adult
$4.50, seniors
$2.50, ages 6 - 18
Ages 5 and under, free
Group rates available

FACILITIES
Gift Shop
Nature trail
Parking (free)
Pets allowed on leash
Picnic area with grills
Restrooms
Visitors Center including brochures, video presentation, museum

SPECIAL EVENTS
Special programs occur throughout the year. Call or check the website for details.

HINTS
* Bug spray and sunscreen during warm months
* Plan a meal for this outing, either a picnic or a restaurant in Darien
* Check special events and time your visits accordingly

"I like learning about history. I would like to go to the Colonial Christmas."

Ansley Guthrie, age 9

"I like the cannons."

Darr Smith, age 9

Fort King George today is a replica of the original structure built in 1721, about twelve years before the colony of Georgia was established at Savannah. Located at the mouth of the Altamaha River, this fortification was proposed by Col. John Barnwell of South Carolina to safeguard the land from the French and Spanish. Although it was in service only for a short time, from 1721 to 1732, Fort King George asserted the British presence along Georgia's coastal corridor.

Visitors enter through the Museum, which includes a film about the early inhabitants of the area, the construction of the fort, and the lives of those garrisoned here. Though there were no major battles fought here, there were many deaths caused by disease and malnutrition. The Museum features exhibits of the site's inhabitants through several centuries. There is a display of 18th century medical instruments used in the fort's infirmary that will be of interest to curious youngsters.

The fort and its buildings can be reached either by a trail that meanders along the marsh or by a more direct route straight from the museum. Children will want to hurry ahead to see this unusual structure enclosed within a moat and a palisade fence.

Built in the style of a European fortified outpost, Fort King George, named for King George I, was designed for defense. The complex of buildings is small in scale and includes the moat and palisade fence, a parapet to defend against land attacks, four sentry boxes, cannon emplacements along the river, and the most prominent structure, the Blockhouse. Other buildings include barracks for soldiers and officers, an infirmary that was originally intended to be a guardhouse, a blacksmith shop and a bakery. Children will enjoy wandering around and through the structures, especially the multi-storied blockhouse with its loophole windows and views of the river and mainland. A ladder on the river side invites climbers into a high opening, so be watchful of very young children.

The soldiers garrisoned here suffered from insects, extremes of heat and humidity, disease and poor diet. Those who survived returned to South Carolina in 1727, leaving two people to keep watch for invaders. In 1736, Highland Scots were sent by General Oglethorpe to Fort King George, but later moved upriver to a new settlement that became the town center of Darien.

Fort King George attracts 40,000 visitors annually, and signs throughout Darien point the way to the site. Comfortable shoes are recommended; the ground can be soggy. Allow one and one-half hours for your visit, and consider combining with a trip to nearby Hofwyl-Broadfield Plantation or the Altamaha Waterfowl Management Area.

HARRIS NECK NATIONAL WILDLIFE REFUGE

Owned and managed by U.S. Fish and Wildlife Service
1000 Business Center Drive
Parkway Business Center, Suite 10
Savannah, Georgia 31305
(912) 652-4415
Refuge Location: Harris Neck Road (Highway 131)
Off U.S. Highway 17 between Eulonia and Darien,
    in McIntosh County, GA (From I-95 take Exit 67)
www.fws.gov/harrisneck/

- -

DAYS/HOURS OF OPERATION
7 days per week, sunrise to sundown

ADMISSION
Free

FACILITIES
Handicapped accessible - some trails
Restrooms
Trails for hiking, bicycling and driving
Visitor Center

HINTS
* Call or visit the website for calendar of seasonal activities
* Take plenty of drinking water, sunscreen, bug spray and hats
* Plan ahead for biking, fishing, crabbing, boating
* Combine with a visit to the "Smallest Church in America"

"I want to see all the birds and I like to fish."
Grace Guthrie, age 7

"I would like to go fishing and watch the birds feed."
Hunter Smith, age 7

Harris Neck National Wildlife Refuge, one of seven refuges in the coastal system, accommodates explorers in cars, on bicycles or on foot. Whether you are seeking a leisurely drive through beautiful scenery or a more active outing with biking, hiking, fishing or crabbing, Harris Neck is a great place to see wildlife and nature in abundance.

Harris Neck's history includes production of sea island cotton and other agricultural uses. Much of the acreage was condemned at the beginning of World War II by the U.S. Government for use as an army air base. Remains of the runways and foundations of service buildings are still visible. In 1962, the land was acquired as a migratory bird refuge.

Just inside the entrance is an informational kiosk and a small dock. Follow the road to the staffed Visitors Center, where there are posters, brochures, restrooms and a water fountain.

You will see saltwater marshes, freshwater ponds, forested areas and open, grassy fields. Well-marked trails of varying distances are easy to navigate. Many species of birds are seen year-round. Deer, turkey, hogs and alligators roam the refuge, so be sure to accompany young children at all times. There are two boat ramps and fishing piers for saltwater fishing and crabbing (licenses required), so plan ahead to ensure supplies and gear.

Be sure to bring drinking water and sunscreen. A picnic will fill the time, but must be consumed tailgate-style, with all food items carried away when you leave. This is a great place for bicycles.

Call ahead or visit the website to take advantage of seasonal offerings, such as the Christmas Bird Count in December or the Butterfly survey in July.

While in the area, stop in and see the "Smallest Church in America." Located on Highway 17 about one mile south of I-95 exit 67, this tiny building was built in 1949 by a local grocer. Measuring 10 X 15 feet, the church holds 13 people and is probably smaller than a child's bedroom. A snapshot of children standing next to the tiny sanctuary will be fun to look at in later years.

HOFWYL-BROADFIELD PLANTATION HISTORIC SITE

Owned and managed by the Georgia Department of Natural
  Resources, State Parks & Historic Sites Division
5566 U.S. Highway 17 North
Brunswick, GA 31525
(912) 264-7333
www.gastateparks.org/info/hofwyl

- -

DAYS/HOURS OF OPERATION
Tuesday-Saturday: 9 a.m. - 5 p.m.
Sunday: 2 p.m. - 5:30 p.m.
Closed Monday (except holidays), Christmas, Thanksgiving
        and New Year's Day

ADMISSION
$5 per adult
$2.50, ages 6 - 18
$4.50, ages 62 and older
Group rates for 15 or more people
  with advance reservations:
$3.50 per person for adults,
    $2.00 per person for students/children

FACILITIES
Gift Shop
Guided house tour
Handicapped accessible (first floor of house)
Leashed pets allowed on grounds
Parking (free)
Picnic area
Restrooms
Soft drink machine
Trail
Visitor's Center including brochures, video presentation, museum

HINTS

* Allow 1.5 hours
* Take snacks or a picnic
* Bug spray and sunscreen during warmer months
* Lots of open space for running and roaming

"My favorite time to visit Hofwyl-Broadfield is at Christmas, because you get to learn about colonial Christmases."

Augusta Eswine, age 10

Hofwyl-Broadfield Plantation is a reminder of a time long ago when generations of one family lived in the same house. This concept seems odd in today's faster-paced, on-the-go lifestyles. Five generations of the Brailsford-Troup-Dent family lived here from its establishment around 1800 as a rice plantation until 1973, when Miss Ophelia Dent, the last family member, departed, leaving the property to the State of Georgia.

The centerpiece of this plantation is the house, which appears exactly as it did when Miss Ophelia lived here. You can almost hear her walking down the hallway.

Begin your visit at the Visitor's Center, enjoying a 17-minute film about the family, the house and the agricultural practices from rice plantation to dairy farm. Hofwyl-Broadfield represents one family's determination to keep its land productive and profitable during changing times and economies. The Visitor's Center also has a model of the working plantation, exhibits about the rice culture, and artifacts from the house and grounds.

From the Visitor's Center, enjoy a pleasant stroll through a grove of live oaks and across a field to the house. Guided tours begin each hour from the screened porch. If you have a wait, wander around the house and its outbuildings, which include an ice house, a dairy barn, a pay station and house servant's quarters. You can also enjoy the view of the marsh and the river beyond.

Hofwyl-Broadfield guides lead you through the house room by room, and they are adept at engaging the interest and attention of young people. Children and adults alike will be curious about the quarantine room, the size and scale of the furnishings and other "oddities" that speak of an earlier time in history.

Allow about one and a half hours for a full visit here. When approaching the entrance on Highway 17, note that it is more visible to northbound travelers than southbound. Consider combining a visit to Hofwyl-Broadfield with one of the other sites in this area-the St. Simons' Lighthouse, Altamaha Waterfowl Management Area or Fort King George.

SAPELO ISLAND

Owned and operated by Georgia Department of Natural Resources
Location: Ga. Highway 99, Meridian, GA,
   8 miles northeast of Darien
Mailing: Route 1, Box 1500, Darien, GA 31305
912-437-3224 (reservations)
912-485-2251 (group tours)
www.gastateparks.org/info/sapelo/

DAYS/HOURS OF OPERATION

Visitors Center: Tuesday - Friday, 7:30 a.m. - 5:30 p.m.
   Saturday, 8 a.m. - 5:30 p.m.; Sunday, 1:30 - 5 p.m.
Ferry schedule and Island visits: Wednesdays and Fridays, 8:30 - 12:30
   By pre-arrangement only

ADMISSION

$10 per adult
$6 children ages 6 to 18 Children under 5, free

FACILITIES

Camping
Mainland Visitors Center
On-island restaurant

HINTS

* Plan a full day
* Call ahead for special tours

"The lighthouse is red and white and I like it here.
I want to do a camping trip with my daddy.
It is pretty on the island."

Hunter Smith, age 7

Sapelo Island has been called home by Guale Indians, Spanish missionaries, French royalists and some of America's best known millionaires. Today Sapelo is home to a small population of researchers and a resident African-American community, who enjoy life on this remote barrier island, one of several which protect the Georgia coast.

Operated by the Georgia Department of Natural Resources, the island is a National Estuarine Research Reserve that welcomes visitors who want to see the diversity of coastal habitats. It is the fourth largest barrier island in Georgia, eleven miles long and two to four miles wide. Sapelo is accessible only by ferry.

Familiar millionaires who have owned Sapelo land are Thomas Spalding, Howard Coffin and R. J. Reynolds. The island retains significant vestiges and landmarks from each family's period of ownership. Perhaps most notable is the Reynolds mansion, which contains a bowling alley and an indoor swimming pool.

A Sapelo adventure is a full day, from leaving to returning home, so plan diversions for drive time. The Sapelo ferry leaves Meridian, GA (just north of Darien) at specified hours. The mainland visitor center will keep children busy with exhibits, and the 30-minute ferry ride builds anticipation. All visitors must have a reservation. Individuals can call 912-437-3224 to set up a sponsor and guide who will meet you on the island. Group tours and special field trips can be booked by calling 912-485-2300.

A video presentation about the island is shown in the Research Lab. This is a good overview of island history, flora and fauna, the coastal ecosystem and earlier inhabitants. Your visit may include a trip to Behavior Cemetery, the residential neighborhood of Hog Hammock, the largest grass airstrip in Georgia, the Sapelo lighthouse, a drive by the Reynolds mansion and a trip to the beach. Special arrangements can be made for seine netting and other special activities.

Camping for groups of 15 or more is available through the state for a minimum of two nights with advance reservations. Call (912) 485-2299 for information. A local resident offers camping for families. Call (912) 485-2170 for more information.

Sapelo is full of history and opportunities for adventure. The ferry ride back to the mainland and the drive home are likely to be nap times for youngsters. Bug spray, sunscreen, hats and visors, towels, drinks and snacks are "musts" for a Sapelo outing.

ST. SIMONS AND JEKYLL ISLANDS

1. Fort Frederica National Monument
2. Jekyll Island
   Jekyll Island Welcome Center
3. Maritime Center at the Historic Coast Guard Station
4. St. Simons Island Lighthouse Museum

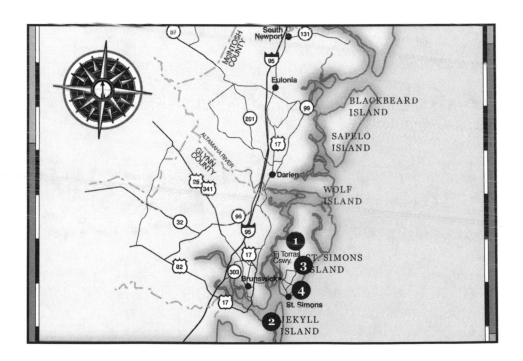

FORT FREDERICA
NATIONAL MONUMENT

Mailing Address:
Route 9, Box 286C
St. Simons Island, Georgia   31522-9710

Location Address:
6515 Frederica Road
St. Simons Island, GA 31522
(912) 638-3639
www.nps.gov/fofr

■■

DAYS/HOURS OF OPERATION
7 days a week: 8 a.m. to 5 p.m.
Visitors Center Hours: 9 a.m. to 5 p.m.

ADMISSION
$3 per adult (age 16 and up)
Under 16, free
Park Pass Discounts

FACILITIES
Brochures
Drink Machines
Film
Gift Shop

Handicapped Access (Golf carts are available with some notice)
Museum
Parking
Pets allowed on leash
Restrooms
Self-guided tour

HINTS
* Allow two hours for visit
* Visit website for information on Special Events

"This place is neat, like a ghost town."

Joe Ratterree, age 9

"I like to pretend the streets and houses are still here."

Katie Ratterree, age 5

If you are near St. Simons Island, allow time for the relaxing drive to the historic north end of the island for a visit to Fort Frederica. Here General James Edward Oglethorpe founded a strategically-located frontier town on the banks of the Frederica River. Claiming the colony of Georgia for the British, Oglethorpe established this military outpost in 1754 to defend from Spanish challenge the newly claimed land of Georgia.

First, an earthenwork fort was built, loaded with cannon and soldiers. Next, a military town was laid out on the bluff, standing watch for any threat from the Spanish in the south. The town and river were named for Frederick, King George II's only son. The town was fortified next by a tabby fort, remnants of which can still be seen.

In June, 1742, the Battle of Bloody Marsh was decisively won by the British, sending the Spanish farther south. By 1745, the town was secured and flourishing. Streets were laid out, houses were built and occupied, crops were planted, soldiers drilled on the parade grounds, and artisans were busy crafting the new community. Unfortunately for the town of Frederica, Oglethorpe's regiment was disbanded in 1749. Without the military economy, the town quickly fell into decline and by 1755, the town of Frederica had become a "ghost town."

Today, Fort Frederica invites visitors to a leisurely stroll down imaginary streets, where foundations of centuries-old houses are exposed. A few Seville orange trees still grow on the site, remnants of earlier Spanish residents. Children will enjoy standing on the raised mounds of the early British fort on the banks of the river, picturing the ominous possibility of a Spanish flag flying from the mast of an approaching warship.

Brick and tabby ruins are scattered throughout the site. The National Park Service engages visitors in the only opportunity on the coast to observe a clear demonstration of how to make tabby. Oyster shells were burned to make lime, then mixed with mud and shells to form tabby, the most common building material for constructing lowcountry dwellings.

Lots of interpretive signs are scattered throughout the site which help children and adults clearly picture life in this pre-Revolutionary town.

The Museum and Visitors Center offers a quick overview of the fort with a 25-minute film. Displays of artifacts found on the site and a model of the fort are also fun to see. Maps for self-guided tours are available inside the Visitors Center. During the summer (and depending on staffing), children will enjoy a hands-on musket drill. Staff and volunteers dress as British soldiers, following the traditional routine of a soldier in the 1740s. Call ahead to find out when these demonstrations are scheduled.

Christ Episcopal Church, founded in 1736, stands within the old walls of Fort Frederica, but a little distance from the parking lot of the Fort. Charles Wesley was the first minister at Frederica and also served as Oglethorpe's Secretary for Indian Affairs.

Across the street from the church is a short nature walk which leads to the Wesley Garden. The short walk and garden commemorate the ministry of John and Charles Wesley who were both in this area at various times in the mid-1700s.

JEKYLL ISLAND
JEKYLL ISLAND WELCOME CENTER

901 Downing Musgrove Causeway
Jekyll Island, GA 31527
(877) 4JEKYLL or (912) 635-3636
www.jekyllisland.com

- -

DAYS/HOURS OF OPERATION
7 days a week: 9 a.m. to 5 p.m.

ADMISSION
$3 per car to access island

FACILITIES
Biking Paths
Boat Ramp
Fishing with permit
Handicapped Access
Hotels
Nature Center
Parking
Pets on leash
Picnic areas
Restaurants
Restrooms
Special Events
Trails

HINTS
* Sunscreen, hats, bug spray
* Plan an overnight for more time to visit

"Jekyll Island has wide beaches that are great
for finding seashells. Also there are lots of bike trails
so bring your bicycle."

Augusta Eswine, age 10

Jekyll Island is one of four barrier islands on the Georgia coast that is accessible by car. Driving over the long causeway to Jekyll, visitors will enjoy the views of the expansive and beautiful marshes of Glynn, made famous by poet Sidney Lanier in the 1800s. Visitors will also appreciate why so few of Georgia's barrier islands are easily accessible. Georgia has wide stretches of marsh which are full of meandering creeks which separate the mainland from the barrier islands.

A three-dollar entrance fee is charged for all visitors to the island. The Welcome Center on the Causeway, located just before the entrance booth, keeps regular hours of 8 a.m. to 5 p.m., and will help orient first-time visitors to the island. Underneath the bridge to the island is a great wildlife viewing area for birds and dolphins.

As a barrier island, Jekyll is home to abundant wildlife - deer, armadillos, raccoons, opossums, shorebirds, migrating hawks and songbirds.

Visitors to the island may want to begin at Millionaire's Village, the first left after the ticket gate.

The first human residents on Jekyll were the Indians who left little or no impact on the land. The next human residents were the Spanish, who named the island the Isla de las Ballenas (the Island of Whales). They must have known about the calving grounds of the Northern Atlantic Right Whale off Georgia's coast, a fact lost, then rediscovered and documented in the 1980s. The pregnant female Right Whales migrate from New England to the gentle Georgia waters to give birth in the winter months. Sightings of the whales are rare, however, because this species is in serious decline.

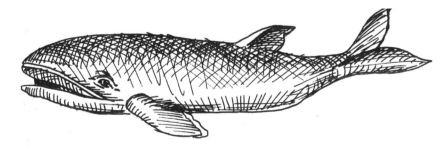

After the Spanish were conquered, the area was populated by English colonial settlers and African-Americans in the 1700s. The oldest structure on the island is the ruin of the Horton House, built in the 1730s.

In 1886, a group of millionaires purchased the island and founded the original Jekyll Island Club. The island became a favorite retreat for America's wealthiest families such as the Astors, Morgans, Rockefellers, Pulitzers, Goulds, and Vanderbilts.

The Jekyll Island National Historic Landmark District can be toured by car, but visitors will experience more of the Village on foot or by a train/shuttle tour. The Historic District encompasses 240 acres with 33 historic structures utilized now as museums, gift shops, restaurants, and a luxury hotel.

Signs directing visitors to the Jekyll Island Museum are easy to follow, and this is a good first stop. Tours aboard a trolley are offered three or four times a day. Biking and footpaths are easily accessed from here. Exhibits located in the old carriage house orient new visitors to the Historic District and the Island.

The Museum serves also as the origination spot for Carriage Rides and even trail rides on horseback. Evening tours and moonlight rides are also possible, but all of these special tours require advance reservations. Call (912) 635-9500 for more information.

Allow at least two hours for touring the Jekyll Island Club's Historic Landmark District. Beautiful live oaks provide shaded walkways and bike paths to this Gatsby-era millionaire's village. The café at the Club Hotel serves ice cream, cold drinks, soup, sandwiches, and cookies in an informal setting.

Adjacent to the club is the newly opened Georgia Sea Turtle Center, a one-of-a-kind in Georgia. Children will enjoy visiting this rehabilitation center for injured sea turtles. For information and hours of operation visit www.georgiaseaturtles.org.

Driving north from the Historic Landmark District, visitors can make a complete loop of the island on the paved road called Riverview Drive which turns into Beachview Drive.

Possible stops along this circular route include:

* The Horton House ruins, dating from 1742.
* The Clam Creek picnic and camping area which also has a covered fishing pier.
* Jekyll's front beach with hotels, restaurants, convention center, miniature golf, beachcombing, picnicking, swimming, and public restrooms. The beachfront pavilion serves ice cream and cold drinks.
* The South Dunes Picnic Area near the Soccer Complex on the south end.
* The St. Andrews Beach and 4-H Club Camp on the south end.
* The St. Andrews Picnic Area with great views of the St. Andrews Sound behind the island.

149

* A recycling center.
* Summer Waves Water Park, expensive but always popular with the children.
* Tidelands Nature Center, a University of Georgia 4-H Program. Kayak programs run from here. Hours are Monday - Friday, 9 a.m. to 4 p.m., Saturday - Sunday, 10 a.m. to 2 p.m. Located on a freshwater pond with dock. The boat ramp is just past the pond and will access the back river.

With so many activities available, your family may want to plan an overnight at Jekyll. There are several hotels to choose from on the front of the Island and the more luxurious Jekyll Island Club Hotel on the back river. A fall or winter visit to the beach can be as much fun as a summer visit. Seasonal prices are more affordable, the weather is cooler for outdoor activities, and bugs are less noticeable!

MARITIME CENTER AT THE HISTORIC COAST GUARD STATION

4201 First Street, East Beach
St. Simons Island, GA
(912) 638-4666, Georgia Historical Society
www.saintsimonslighthouse.org/maritime.html

- -

DAYS/HOURS OF OPERATION
Monday-Saturday: 10 a.m. to 5 p.m.
Sunday: 1:30 - 5 p.m.
Closed Major Holidays

ADMISSION
$6 per adult
$3 children over 5
Children under 5, Free
Combination Ticket for Lighthouse and Maritime Center,
    $10 Adult/$6 Children

FACILITIES
Beach Volleyball
Drink Machine
Gift shop
Handicapped Access
Parking
Restrooms

HINTS
* Combine with a visit to the Lighthouse
* Parking is plentiful with easy access to beach
* Allow an hour for complete tour

The Maritime Center is located in the historic Coast Guard Station which was built in 1936. This Station was part of the Roosevelt-era WPA project, and was one of 45 coast guard stations erected across the United States in the 1930s. Only a few still stand. The station was actively used by the Coast Guard until 1995, and is now beautifully restored as a Maritime Center with interactive exhibits on two floors.

Opened in 2006, the Center welcomes visitors from the front porch which faces the ocean. A small gift shop is on the right where admission fees are collected. Rooms are spacious and exhibits on the first floor illustrate training in the Coast Guard and the dynamic nature of the sands on barrier islands. There is also a small theatre on the first floor with a 12-minute film on St. Simons Island that runs continually.

Upstairs exhibits cover weather, marsh, the work of the Coast Guard, and World War II and its influence on St. Simons Island.

The Maritime Center is conveniently located adjacent to public access to the beach with plenty of parking.

THE MEMORY GAME

FOR TWO OR MORE PLAYERS

Look around you carefully. Try to notice every detail of your surroundings. Now close your eyes and get ready to test your memory! Get your friend to ask you a question such as: "Is there a shark in a painting on the wall?" or maybe a trickier question such as: "What color is the chair in the corner?" You may keep score and add a point when you get a question right and subtract a point if you miss one. You may take turns asking the questions.

Created and written by Mary Ellen McKee, age 11

ST. SIMONS ISLAND LIGHTHOUSE AND MUSEUM

Owned and managed by Coastal Georgia Historical Society
P.O. Box 21136
101 12th Street
St. Simons Island, GA 31522-0636
(912) 638-4666
www.saintsimonslighthouse.org

DAYS/HOURS OF OPERATION
Monday through Saturday: 10 a.m. - 5 p.m.
Sundays: 1:30 p.m. - 5 p.m.
(Lighthouse closes at 4:45 p.m. Allow 30 minutes for complete tour.)

ADMISSION
$5 per adult
$2.50 children under 12
Free, children under 6
Free Admission to Museum Store
Disability Access provided upon request.

FACILITIES
Drink Machine
Gazebo
Museum Shop
Parking
Picnic Area nearby
Restrooms available to paying guests

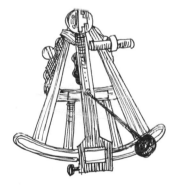

HINTS
* Plan a picnic lunch or lunch in the village, a short walk from
  the lighthouse
* Allow an hour for lighthouse, plus play time in nearby Neptune Park

**"At the St. Simons Lighthouse it is worth the walk up
all those stairs to the top. When you get there the view
is great and there is a strong breeze to cool you off."**

Augusta Eswine, age 10

A 90-minute drive from Savannah, the St. Simons Island Lighthouse is a picturesque and delightful excursion. The village of St. Simons is within walking distance of the lighthouse.

The all white St. Simons lighthouse with intermittent black windows overlooks the Atlantic Ocean and St. Simons Sound, offering one of the best views of Georgia's coast. As symbols, lighthouses are often a spiritual or religious logo. They are symbolic also for their service to all humanity, guiding people to safe ports.

Each lighthouse in the country is distinct, with size and construction guided by specific geographical and navigational dictates. Each lighthouse also has distinctive daymarks, large painted patterns that distinguish a particular lighthouse when it is visible from the sea.

The first lighthouse at St. Simons was built in 1807, but it was destroyed in 1862 by the Confederate Army so Union forces could not use it as a navigational aid.

The second lighthouse, the one currently in use and open to the public, was constructed in 1872. The 104 foot tower has 129 steps in a cast-iron spiral staircase. The view is spectacular from the top, and it is very safe. Visitors are allowed to go out on the walkway. Children will see large ships entering and leaving the harbor and perhaps even glimpse a large school of dolphin in the St. Simons Sound. Strong winds and rain may close the tower, so if there is a question about the weather, be sure to call before you go.

A good time to visit would be earlier in the morning, as the lighthouse itself is not air conditioned, although the adjacent keeper's cottage and museum are delightfully cool. This still-operating lighthouse beacon can be seen 23 miles out to sea.

The Lighthouse Museum is operated by the Coastal Georgia Historical Society, and includes a gift shop in which lighthouses are featured prominently on umbrellas, stationery, magnets, gift wrapping, postcards, kaleidoscopes, and T-shirts. Near the lighthouse is Neptune Park with picnic tables in the shade of two magnificent canopied live oaks. A wonderful sculpture of a right whale mother and calf is located nearby as well as a playground and covered deck on the sound with benches and a delightful view. There is also a pier where fishing is free.

OTHER DAY TRIPS OUTSIDE
OF CHATHAM COUNTY

■■

1. The Center for Wildlife Education and
    The Lamar Q. Ball, Jr. Raptor Center
    (Bulloch County)
2. Fort McAllister State Historic Site
    (Bryan County)
3. New Ebenezer Church and Museum
    (Effingham County)

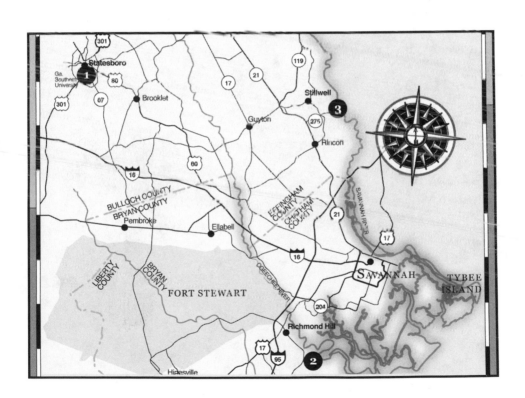

THE CENTER FOR WILDLIFE EDUCATION & THE LAMAR Q. BALL, JR. RAPTOR CENTER

Forest Drive in Statesboro,
    just inside Georgia Southern University entrance
    on Highway 301
Mailing: P. O. Box 8058
    Statesboro, GA 30460
912-681-0831
ceps.georgiasouthern.edu/wildlife

■■■

DAYS/HOURS OF OPERATION
Monday - Friday: 9 a.m. to 5 p.m.
Saturday - Sunday: 1 to 5 p.m.

ADMISSION
Free for walk-ins
Groups of 10 or more with a program:
    $2.50 Pre-K, $3.00 Kindergarten and older

FACILITIES
Drink machines and water fountains
Handicapped accessible
Parking
Picnic area and shelter
Restrooms
Trails
Visitor Center and Gift Shop

SPECIAL EVENTS
Birthday parties
Group programs available for specialized and general field trips
Overnight and evening programs
Summer camps

HINTS
* Bug spray
* Allow at least one hour
* Bring a snack or picnic

"This is one of my favorite places because I like the outdoors and birds in the woods."

Landon Kight, Claxton, age 7

"I like lions and tigers but I haven't seen any here."

Page Kight, Claxton, age 3

"I have a pet turtle named Franklin so I like to come see the turtles."

Justin Barefoot, Pooler, age 8

Just inside the Georgia Southern University campus in Statesboro is a twelve-acre site where children can meet face-to-face with birds of prey and other Georgia wildlife. The Center for Wildlife Education and the Lamar Q. Ball, Jr. Raptor Center opened in 1997 as an environmental education resource.

Here you will find not only gopher tortoises and snakes, but also a variety of predatory birds in habitats that mimic Georgia's diverse land forms. Barn owls, peregrine falcons, a great horned owl, a red-shouldered hawk and a bald eagle reside here. These raptors are unable for various reasons to live in the wild, but when viewed in their settings here you may forget that they cannot fly away.

Check in at the Visitor Center where you will receive a brochure and enjoy an indoor exhibit of Georgia wildlife. Ask for activity handouts that will keep young minds focused on discovering. There is a Gift Shop here as well, which you will want to save until the end of your visit.

Outside, two trails await adventurers. Signage throughout the site provides useful information. The Habitat Walk is a wooden boardwalk through hills and mountains, the forest edge, wetlands, an old growth forest and other habitats, each featuring live birds of prey. Children will enjoy seeing a bald eagle on her nest from the top of the boardwalk.

The Discovery Trail is a paved path embossed with the footprints of various "critters." This trail includes discovery boxes of wildlife artifacts such as owl pellets, raptor feathers and turtle shells, as well as a striped skunk, an opossum and other animals in small habitats.

An amphitheatre seating 120 people is the perfect outdoor classroom for groups. During the week, flight demonstrations by trained falconers are held for reserved groups. Walk-in visitors who happen to be here at those times are welcome to join the group. On Saturdays, visitors can enjoy a reptile demonstration at 2 p.m. and a Flight Show at 3 p.m. When the outdoor air temperature is 85 degrees or greater, the flight shows are held inside.

Located about one hour from Savannah, this site is well worth the travel time for a fun outing.

FORT MCALLISTER STATE HISTORIC SITE

3894 Fort McAllister Road
Richmond Hill, GA 31324
912-727-2339
912-727-3614
www.fortmcallister.org

■■

DAYS/HOURS OF OPERATION
Every day: 8 a.m. - 5 p.m.
Closed Thanksgiving and Christmas

ADMISSION
$3 per car for entry to the fort, park, playground and fishing pier
$4 per adult, $2.50 for children, $3.50 senior citizens
    for admission to the historic site

FACILITIES
Drink Machine
Gift Shop
Museum and Theatre
Nature Trail
Picnic area
Restrooms

SPECIAL EVENTS
Memorial Day, Fourth of July, Labor Day
Candle Lantern Tour, October
Winter Muster, December

HINTS
* Bug spray, hats and sunscreen
* Plan to include a meal or snacks
* 30 to 45 minute drive from Savannah

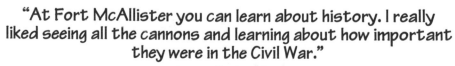

"At Fort McAllister you can learn about history. I really
liked seeing all the cannons and learning about how important
they were in the Civil War."

Augusta Eswine, age 10

Located on the Ogeechee River just outside Richmond Hill, Fort McAllister is a great adventure both for Civil War history buffs and those who simply want to enjoy a great coastal outing.

Historical records point to Guale Indian inhabitants as early as 3000 BC, and the naturalist William Bartram passed through in 1750. Other visitors of note include Robert E. Lee and William Tecumseh Sherman.

Today the fort is best known for its place in Civil War history. Fort McAllister was strategically located to defend the Georgia coastal plantations and particularly the railroads. Landowner Joseph McAllister offered his land for the construction of Confederate earthworks. In 1862, the *CSS Nashville* eluded the Union blockade and arrived at McAllister. Ultimately, the *Nashville*, renamed the *Rattlesnake*, was defeated by the *USS Montauk*, and sank off shore where its hull still remains.

The *Nashville* may have been lost, but the fort's earthen mounds, constructed to defend attacks from the river, successfully resisted bombardment from the Union ironclads. However, never intended to defend against attacks on land, McAllister fell quickly to Sherman's ground troops, thus ending the Union general's March to the Sea in 1864.

Begin your visit at the Museum and enjoy a short film about the fort. The real fun begins outdoors, where children will gain entry by crossing a moat of sharpened, upended palisades. Cannons and guns are positioned along the river and around the fort. A favorite for youngsters is the hot shot gun, whose hot cannon balls ignited wooden vessels. The large earthen mounds reveal rooms beneath, including the huge Center Bombproof that was a refuge during bombardment and a hospital.

The fort also has a nature trail and lots of room to run around. For those who tire of history, there is a nearby park with a playground and fishing pier.

NEW EBENEZER CHURCH AND MUSEUM

2887 Ebenezer Road
Rincon, GA 31326
912-754-9242
www.newebenezer.org

■■■

DAYS/HOURS OF OPERATION
Museum Hours: Wednesday, Saturday and Sunday, 3 to 5 p.m.,
    or by appointment

ADMISSION
Donations requested

FACILITIES
Museum
Restroom
Trail

HINTS
* Call ahead first to be sure of hours
* Plan a picnic
* Take bug spray and water in summer

"I really like to hike on the trail."
Anne Lillian Bordeaux, age 6

"I like how the cabins are rusty [rustic]."
Thomas Bordeaux, age 5

The historic Ebenezer settlement at Red Bluff offers a view of the Savannah River quite different from the active shipping corridor we see in Savannah. A thirty-mile drive west of Savannah on Highway 21 leads to Ebenezer Road, which ends at the outpost settled by Austrian Salzburgers in 1736. General Oglethorpe led the Salzburgers here, and a town was developed around four squares, similar to Savannah's town plan.

Visitors should begin at the Museum, which gives a history of the settlement and sets the stage for what you will see. Be sure to pick up a Walking Tour Guide ($1.50) for your self-guided tour. Other structures on the site include a cane grinding mill, syrup pot, and a 1755 farmhouse, its separate kitchen connected by a walkway, and the parsonage dating to the 1850s.

An amphitheater is located behind the two houses, right on the banks of the Savannah River. The view is lovely and picnic tables are nearby when meal time arrives. Every Labor Day, New Ebenezer holds an annual cane-grinding with colonial crafts and other special events. Beside the grinding mill is a large open shed called the "Syrup Pot." In the center of the shed is a large circular brick hearth for processing the syrup with the biggest cooking pot your children will ever see.

The Jerusalem Lutheran Church, completed in 1769, is the oldest structure in Georgia. The church has walls that are 21 inches thick that were made from nearby clay. The women and children helped dig the clay and form the bricks, which were fired and used to build the church. Tell your children to stand facing the front doors of the church, then to walk a little to the left and go up close near the left-hand corner of the church. On a child's eye level, if they look very closely, the hand print of a child can be seen in one of the bricks.

The regular hours of operation are somewhat limited on a weekly basis, but tours will be given by appointment with advanced arrangement by calling the Georgia Salzburger Society at 912-754-7001.

In addition to the historic New Ebenezer grounds, there is the New Ebenezer Retreat Center and cemetery across the street. Visitors may want to inquire about this center for future group visits.

CHATHAM COUNTY BARRIER ISLANDS ACCESSIBLE ONLY BY BOAT

1. Ossabaw Island
2. Wassaw Island National Wildlife Refuge

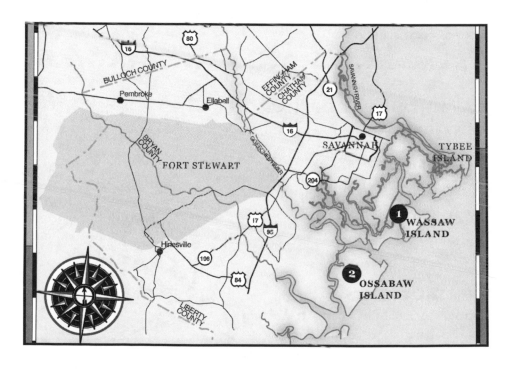

OSSABAW ISLAND

Managed by Georgia Department of Natural Resources
Wildlife Resources Division
22814 Highway 144
Richmond Hill, GA 31324
(912) 727-2112
http://crd.dnr.state.ga.us

Ossabaw Island Foundation
145 Bull Street
Savannah, GA 31401
(912) 233-5104
www.ossabawisland.org

DAYS/HOURS OF OPERATION
By pre-arrangement only

ADMISSION
Boat Transportation costs

FACILITIES
Restrooms
Trails

SPECIAL EVENTS
October Annual Pig Roast/Art Auction,
    Ossabaw Island Foundation
Hunting (seasonal). Contact GA DNR
Camping, by permit only

HINTS
*Bring all the food, water, supplies, and gear you will
  need for a day
*This is a full-day experience. Don't plan anything else
  for the day you visit. You will be tired when you get home!

"I like the donkeys. I like seeing the wild pigs.
I like to play in the trees and swing on the low hanging limbs.
I like the boat ride to Ossabaw."

Selden Frissell, age 6

Ossabaw Island, the southernmost barrier island in Chatham County, meets her visitors with spectacular scenery, rich history, and wildlife that defines itself on each visit. Donkeys, pigs, and horses roam the island, remnants of domestic farming. Wildlife is abundant as well, including eagles, wading and shore birds, migrating waterfowl, hawks, owls, deer, turkey, alligators, and other barrier island wildlife.

Located twenty miles south of Savannah, Ossabaw has 11,800 upland acres and thousands of acres of fresh and saltwater marsh. Human settlements on the island have existed for 4000 years, including the Guale Indians, English colonials, 19th century plantations with resident African-American communities, and 20th century industrialists. Ossabaw's total acreage is 25,000 acres which includes miles of beachfront and freshwater ponds.

Most recently, Ossabaw has been owned by Eleanor (Sandy) Torrey West, a dedicated supporter of the creative arts and the environment. Since the 1960s, Ossabaw has provided a haven and rich subject material for writers, artists, photographers, and environmental enthusiasts, thanks to Sandy West and her generous hospitality. Home to the Ossabaw Project (1960s and 70s) and the Genesis Project (1970s), Ossabaw became the State of Georgia's first Heritage Preserve in 1978, when the state purchased most of the island.

State law requires that all of Georgia's barrier island beaches are open to the public during daylight hours. The beach is available for hiking, picnicking, or shelling. Surf fishing requires a permit. The interior of the island is accessible to visitors by permission from the Ossabaw Island Foundation. As a heritage preserve, the island is available for "natural, scientific, and cultural purposes based on environmentally sound practices."

A visit to Ossabaw is a rare treat, but requires advance planning and careful preparation. There are no public shelters on the island, so arrive prepared for all kinds of weather. You must bring your own food and water and leave with your own trash. Older children who enjoy hiking will enjoy a day on Ossabaw, but be prepared to carry young children. If your children enjoy boat rides, hiking, picnics, and wildlife, they will love Ossabaw!

History, nature, water, weather, and charm will leave you dreaming of another island getaway. Georgia's barrier islands are experienced best October through April, when bugs and weather are more cooperative. Bring your camera, binoculars, and a desire to learn. History and nature will be your teachers. Have an enchanting day!

WASSAW ISLAND NATIONAL WILDLIFE REFUGE

Owned and operated by U.S. Fish and Wildlife Service
Parkway Business Center Drive
1000 Business Center Drive, Suite 10
Savannah, GA 31405
(912) 652-4415
www.fws.gov/wassaw
www.stateparks.com/wassaw

Caretta Research Project
P.O. Box 9841
Savannah, GA 31412-0041

■ ■

DAYS/HOURS OF OPERATION
By pre-arrangement only.
Beach: Sun-up to sundown

ADMISSION
Boat transportation costs

FACILITIES
None

SPECIAL EVENTS
Hunting, Camping
Contact US Fish & Wildlife Service

HINTS
*Bring everything you think you'll need
*Plan several weeks ahead
*Check the weather before you leave

"It's the coolest island in the world."
Mary Ellen McKee, age 12

Begin planning your trip to Wassaw Island weeks ahead. You might read the book, Robinson Crusoe, with your children, then plan your own island adventure.

Wassaw Island, a 10,053 acre refuge, is Chatham County's most remote and beautiful beach. Accessible only by boat, Wassaw requires a spirit of adventure and advance planning, but the effort will be rewarded once you land on this undeveloped, forested barrier island.

Hiking, beachcombing, birdwatching, saltwater fishing, and photography are the main activities on Wassaw. Designated as a National Wildlife Refuge in 1969, Wassaw has twenty miles of dirt roads and seven miles of beach. Bird rookeries for egrets and herons are lodged on inland ponds. The threatened loggerhead sea turtles lumber onto the beach at night to lay their eggs in the sand at the high water mark from May until early August. An active sea turtle protection program, the Caretta Project, patrols the beach at night, tagging turtles and nests. Often, eggs are moved into a hatchery to protect them from raccoons, people, and high tides. Turtle "crawls" can sometimes be found on the beach on a summer morning.

Perhaps the best time to visit Wassaw is the late fall or early spring before the bugs are fierce. A wintertime visit on a sunny December day can be perfect. Young children (under 3) will not enjoy the trip as much because walking is the only mode of transportation once you are on the island. You must also carry your food and water, bug spray, rain gear or a change of clothes. You and your children, like Robinson Crusoe, will be "on your own."

If you don't have a boat of your own, some of the marinas offer charter boat services. Swimming and picnicking are permitted on the beach, but open fires and pets are not allowed. To plan your trip, to inquire about a volunteer-guided visit, or for directions to the island, visit the website or call the Refuge office for more information. It will be a visit you will never forget!

ADDITIONAL INFORMATION

■ ■

Readers are advised to call sites before visiting to confirm hours, days, admission fees, and to find out if there are special events taking place.

The Savannah Visitors Center (featured on page 42) is a good "first stop" for visitors.

The following phone numbers and websites may be helpful in guiding readers to events and activities in addition to those occurring at the sites included in the book. Our website is www.savannahwithchildren.com.

Chatham County. . . . . www.chathamcounty.org
   Public Works and Park Services Dept. . . . . (912) 652-6417
City of Savannah. . . . . www.savannahga.gov
   Leisure Services Bureau. . . . . (912) 351-3837
   Cultural Affairs. . . . . (912) 657-6417
Savannah Convention and Visitors Bureau . . . . www.savcvb.com

March 17 is St. Patrick's Day, and Savannah hosts one of the nation's largest parades. The downtown area is recommended that day only for those who wish to enjoy the parade, as many museums and sites in the area close on this day. Call first to be sure before making plans.

APPENDIX -
LISTING OF SITES BY SUBJECT/THEME

ART

GARDENS

RESTAURANTS IN HISTORIC PLACES

HISTORIC SITES

MUSEUMS

NATURE TRAILS

PARKS, PLAYGROUNDS, OTHER

INDEX